THE ENCYCLOPEDIA OF
NORTH AMERICAN
INDIAN TRIBES

THE ENCYCLOPEDIA OF
NORTH AMERICAN
INDIAN TRIBES

A Comprehensive Study of Tribes from the Abitibi to the Zuni

BILL YENNE

BISON GROUP

Published by
Bison Books Ltd
Kimbolton House
117A Fulham Road
London, SW3 6RL
England

ISBN 0 86124 271 8

Printed in Hong Kong
Reprinted 1989

Page 1: Two Navajo shepherds keep watch over their flock in Monument Valley, located on the Arizona/Utah border. The Navajo call the area 'The Land of Time and Room Enough,' an appropriate name for America's largest reservation.

Title page: Charles M Russell was a prolific artist during the earlier part of this century, and often painted Plains Indians in action. This detail from *Jumped* depicts a surprise attack on a wagon train. Such hit and run warfare was common as the whites moved further into Indian land during the middle to late nineteenth century.

Below: The Taos Pueblo was established centuries ago near the site of present day Santa Fe, New Mexico. It's high-terraced communal dwellings provide a look-out over the smaller Rio Pueblo. The 'beehive' adobe ovens located in the foreground were used by the early Pueblo dwellers for cooking.

Acknowledgments

The author wishes to thank Larry Workman of the Quinault Indian Nation and Gary Robinson of the Muscogee Creek Nation for their help in supplying photographs; and Duane Isham for his work in cataloging the data on individual tribes.

Designed by Bill Yenne and Stephen Spoja

Edited by Susan Garratt

TABLE OF CONTENTS

INTRODUCTION

The Indian tribes of North America are, and have been, as diverse as the vast land in which they live. They range from the hunters and gatherers of the Great Basin, whose lifestyle was almost like that of Stone Age peoples, to the fisherman of the Northwest Coast, who sailed the Pacific in 100-foot galleons and had a tradition of religious and decorative art that rivaled anything else the world had to offer. The tribes range from those that have grown extinct and today have fewer than 50 members to those that have flourished during the twentieth century to more than 50,000 members.

The objective of this encyclopedia is to provide a catalog of the tribes that have existed in North America since prehistoric

Opposite: **A Happy Canyon Princess on horseback, 1985. The parade is part of the Chief Joseph Days, festivities in honor of the Nez Perce chief celebrated in the town named for him.** *Above:* **A typical Haida totem pole at the Lowie Museum of Anthropology, University of California. Sunlight and air have helped preserve these carvings.**

times. For much of the continent the prehistoric period ends with the year AD 1500, although for the Northwest Coast region the year is probably closer to AD 1750. Our survey includes such factors as region, language, dwelling type and subsistence type for each tribe. In all instances these factors are listed as they existed when the tribe first made contact with European civilization. In most cases they probably had been the same for sev-

eral hundred years prior to the start of the historical period, but in many cases they changed dramatically after the arrival of the white man. White settlement and warfare caused certain tribes to abandon ancestral homelands, which in turn brought them into conflict with other tribes. Tribes that suffered from disease and losses in battle merged with other tribes, and original tribal identities were lost. By the early twentieth century many Indian languages fell into disuse and some were lost. The traditional dwelling types listed in our entries gave way to wood-frame houses by the late nineteenth century, although in areas such as the Arctic or the Southwest, for example, the tribes still use traditional housing. Subsistence types had changed considerably by the early twentieth century, and today's reservation grocery store is virtually identical to the type of grocery store in any nearby, non-reservation town or city of comparable size. The Indians of the Plains still hunt big game, but with rifles, and when the Eskimo go out on a seal hunt their boats are powered by gasoline engines.

Much of our fundamental data is based on the work of such noted anthropologists as Harold Driver and Alfred Kroeber, with contemporary population data coming from the US Bureau of Indian Affairs and the Canadian Department of Indian Affairs and Northern Development. We also consulted a variety of other literature and contacted over 100 of the existing North American Indian tribal councils.

In the case of some tribes, data is contradictory and has had to be sorted out through a variety of sources. By the twentieth century many tribes had so few members that they were simply no longer counted, while the Navajo had so many members that they were treated like a fifty-first state.

Some tribes occupy reservations on lands where the tribe has lived for centuries, and other tribes were removed from their traditional lands over a century ago. The tribes of the eastern United States are the most notable of those that no longer live in their traditional homelands. This was the first region in the continent to experience large-scale white settlement, and it was the only region from which there was a large-scale, systematic removal of entire tribes. The tribes of the Northeast were the first to encounter the European immigration, and by the end of the eighteenth century had forfeited much of their land. The tribes of the Southeast and the Great Lakes region of the Northeast, on the other hand, were those most affected by the Indian Removal Act of 1830, which involved the systematic, forced removal of those tribes to west of the Mississippi. In 1837 the US government established Indian Territory, an area comprising what is now Oklahoma, where the tribes removed from east of the Mississippi could be given new lands. The tribes that were first given land in Indian Territory were the five largest tribes from the Southeast: the Cherokee, Chickasaw, Choctaw, Creek and Seminole. These tribes quickly adopted many aspects of European culture, and as a result came to be referred to as the Five Civilized Tribes.

By 1887 so many tribes had been given land within Indian Territory that the US

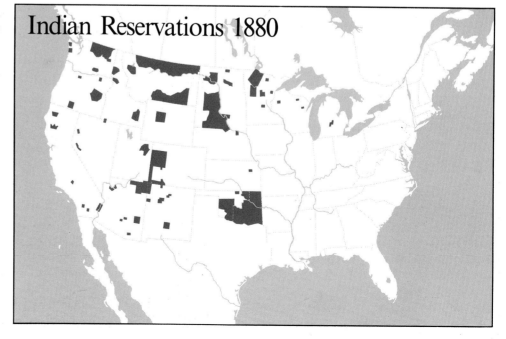

Indian Reservations 1880

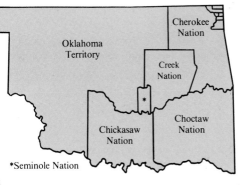

Indian Territory 1891-1907

Indian Territory 1866-1890

Indian Territory 1856-1866

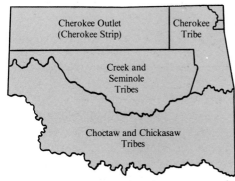

Indian Territory 1837-1855

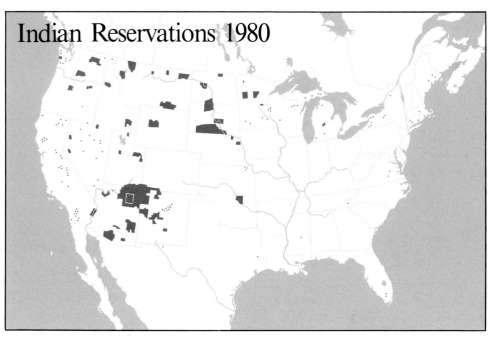

Indian Reservations 1980

Above left: **Residents of New Mexico's Jemez Pueblo perform a Buffalo Dance at an inter-tribal ceremonial.** *Above:* **The evolution of Indian Territory.** *Left:* **In 1880, there were fewer reservations in the United States, but they were bigger than today. The largest (except for Indian Territory) were those of the Blackfoot, Crow and Sioux in Montana and the Dakotas. Today there are more reservations but the land area has dwindled condsiderably. The Navajo Reservation is now the largest, completely surrounding the Hopi Reservation in Arizona. The multitude of small rancheria in California is also visible here.**

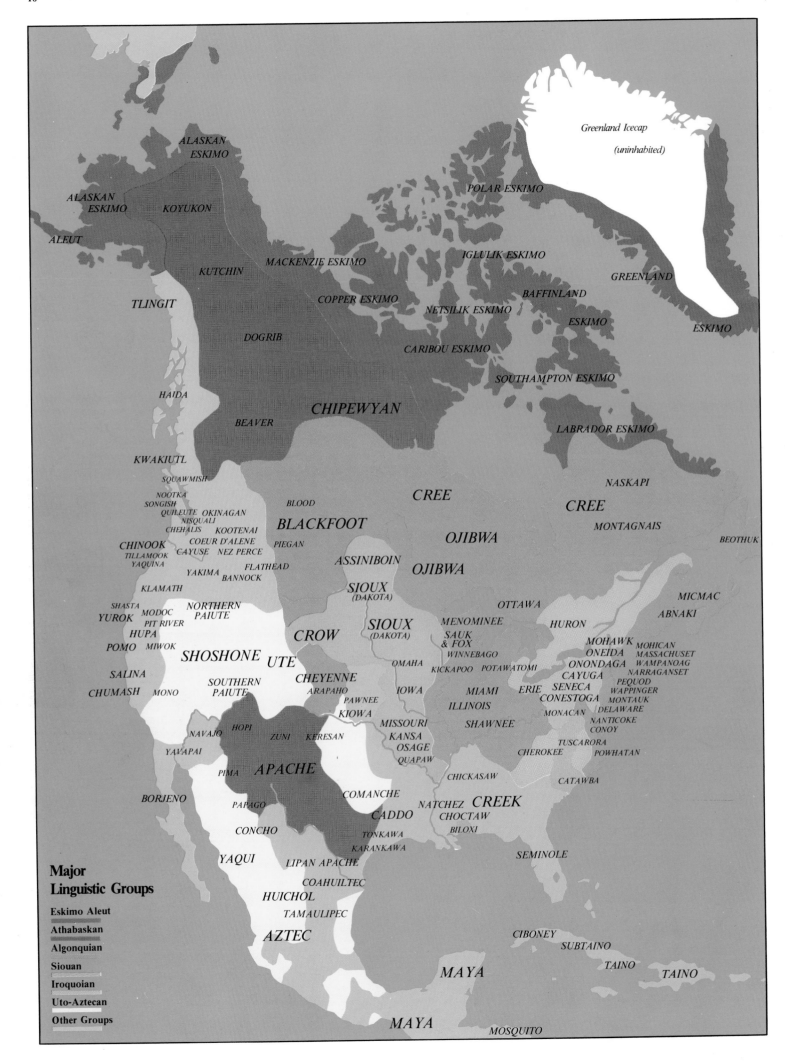

Greenland Icecap

(uninhabited)

ALASKAN ESKIMO

ALASKAN ESKIMO

KOYUKON

POLAR ESKIMO

ALEUT

KUTCHIN

MACKENZIE ESKIMO

IGLULIK ESKIMO

GREENLAND

TLINGIT

COPPER ESKIMO

BAFFINLAND

NETSILIK ESKIMO

ESKIMO

DOGRIB

ESKIMO

CARIBOU ESKIMO

HAIDA

SOUTHAMPTON ESKIMO

CHIPEWYAN

BEAVER

LABRADOR ESKIMO

KWAKIUTL

SQUAWMISH

NASKAPI

NOOTKA

CREE

CREE

SONGISH

BLOOD

QUILEUTE OKINAGAN

BLACKFOOT

MONTAGNAIS

NISQUALI

CHEHALIS

KOOTENAI

OJIBWA

BEOTHUK

CHINOOK

COEUR D'ALENE

PIEGAN

TILLAMOOK

CAYUSE NEZ PERCE

ASSINIBOIN

OJIBWA

YAQUINA

YAKIMA

FLATHEAD

OTTAWA

MICMAC

BANNOCK

KLAMATH

SIOUX

ABNAKI

(DAKOTA)

SHASTA

NORTHERN

MENOMINEE

HURON

YUROK

MODOC

PAIUTE

SIOUX

SAUK

MOHAWK

MOHICAN

PIT RIVER

(DAKOTA)

& FOX

ONEIDA

MASSACHUSET

HUPA

CROW

WINNEBAGO

ONONDAGA

WAMPANOAG

POMO

MIWOK

OMAHA

KICKAPOO

POTAWATOMI

CAYUGA

NARRAGANSET

SALINA

SHOSHONE

UTE

PEQUOD

SENECA

WAPPINGER

SOUTHERN

CHEYENNE

ERIE

CONESTOGA

MONTAUK

CHUMASH

MONO

PAIUTE

ARAPAHO

IOWA

MIAMI

MONACAN

DELAWARE

PAWNEE

ILLINOIS

NANTICOKE

KIOWA

MISSOURI

SHAWNEE

CONOY

NAVAJO

HOPI

ZUNI

KERESAN

KANSA

TUSCARORA

YAVAPAI

OSAGE

CHEROKEE

POWHATAN

PIMA

APACHE

QUAPAW

BORJENO

COMANCHE

CHICKASAW

CATAWBA

PAPAGO

NATCHEZ

CREEK

CONCHO

CADDO

CHOCTAW

YAQUI

TONKAWA

BILOXI

LIPAN APACHE

KARANKAWA

SEMINOLE

COAHUILTEC

HUICHOL

TAMAULIPEC

CIBONEY

AZTEC

SUBTAINO

TAINO

MAYA

TAINO

MAYA

MOSQUITO

Major
Linguistic Groups

Eskimo Aleut

Athabaskan

Algonquian

Siouan

Iroquoian

Uto-Aztecan

Other Groups

government policy was changed, granting land to individual tribe members rather than to the tribe as a whole. By the time Oklahoma became a state in 1906, all of the Indian nations within Indian Territory had been dissolved. Throughout our text, we refer to places by their *current names,* with the exception of Indian Territory for the period from 1837 to 1906.

In other parts of the continent the Indians reacted to white settlement in different ways. Many California Indians adapted readily to life at Spanish missions, while the Plains Indians violently resisted the white encroachment. By 1890 all of the tribes south of Alaska had been placed on reservations, and in 1924 the Indians within the United States were made citizens.

The tribes of North America can be divided into nine specific regions, as noted on the adjacent map. Each of these regions had specific characteristics that set it apart from the other regions, although certain cultural factors, such as language groups, crossed regional borders and others, like the cultivation of maize, were common to several regions. The regional outline given below is greatly simplified, but it does serve to give a concise overview to a complex subject and allow a general understanding of the chief characteristics of the major regions.

The Northeast
Major Language Groups:
    Algonquian and Iroquoian
Dominant Lifestyle: Sedentary
Dominant Tribes:
    Iroquois Confederacy (eastern area)
    Chippewa (Great Lakes area)
Key Food Source: Maize

The Southeast
Major Language Group: Muskogean
Dominant Lifestyle: Sedentary
Dominant Tribes:
    Cherokee, Chickasaw, Choctaw, Creek and Seminole, later referred to as the Five Civilized Tribes
Key Food Source: Maize

California
Major Language Group: Penutian
Dominant Lifestyle: Sedentary
Dominant Tribe: There was no dominant tribe in California. The largest tribes included the Chumash of the south coast and the Hupa, Pomo and Yurok in the north
Key Food Source: Acorns pounded into meal

The Southwest:
Major Language Group:
    Uto-Aztecan/Tanoan
Dominant Tribes and Lifestyles:
    Apache (nomadic)
    Pueblo (sedentary)
    Navajo (sedentary)
Key Food Source: Maize

The Plains
Major Language Group:
    Siouan (northern area)
    Caddoan (Texas)
Dominant Lifestyle: Nomadic
Dominant Tribe: Sioux
Key Food Source: Buffalo

The Northwest Coast
Major Language Groups:
    Salishan/Nadene
Dominant Lifestyle: Sedentary
Dominant Tribes:
    Tlingit (Alaskan panhandle)
    Haida (Queen Charlotte Islands)
    Kwakiutl (British Columbia coast)
    Chinook (northwestern United States coast)
Key Food Source: Salmon

The Great Basin
Major Language Group: Uto-Aztecan
Dominant Lifestyle: Nomadic (except sedentary in the foothills of the Rockies in northern Idaho and northwestern Montana)
Dominant Tribe: Shoshone and related tribes such as Paiute (except in the area between the Columbia River basin and the foothills of the Rockies, where tribes such as Nez Percé and the Spokane predominated)
Key Food Source: Small Game

The Arctic
Major Language Group: Eskimo-Aleut
Dominant Lifestyle:
    Nomadic (summer)
    Sedentary (winter)
Dominant Tribe: Eskimo
Key Food Source: Sea mammals

The Subarctic
Major Language Group: Athapaskan
Dominant lifestyle: Nomadic
Dominant Tribe: Chipewyan
Key Food Source: Caribou

THE ENCYLOPEDIA OF
NORTH AMERICAN
INDIAN TRIBES

Abihki (*see* Creek)

Abitibi, Abitibiwinni
Geographic Region: Northeast (Northeast Ontario)
Linguistic Group: Algonquian
Principal Dwelling Type: Domed bark, thatch or hide house
Principal Subsistence Type: Fish, wild game
At the beginning of 1984, there were 60 Abitibi living on the south shore of Lake Abitibi, Ontario, and 478 Abitibiwinni living near Amos, Quebec.

Abnaki (Abneki, Wabunaki)
Geographic Region: Northeast (New England)
Linguistic Group: Algonquian
Principal Dwelling Type: Crude conical tipi
Principal Subsistence Type: Hunting, maize
The name Abnaki, or more properly Wabunaki, means 'those living at the sunrise,' and is generally applied to the Algonquian peoples living in Maine. They

include the related Penobscot and Passamaquoddy, as well as the Malecite, Arosaguntacock and Sokoki. The Abnaki made contact with whites, particularly the French, in the seventeenth century. After defeats by the English at Norridgewock in 1724, and at Pequawket in 1725, they withdrew to Canada and settled with other refugee tribes at St Francis. They resettled in Maine by 1890 and were observed to have developed the splint type of basket making more common earlier in the western Great Lakes region. In 1967, there were 616 Abnakis in Canada. The 1985 reservation population of Maine was 2918, including 1070 Passamaquoddy and 1106 Penobscot.

Absaroka (*see* Crow)

Absentee Shawnee (*see* Shawnee)

Achumawi (Achomawi)
Geographic Region: Northeast California (Pit River)
Linguistic Group: Hokan-Shasta
Principal Dwelling Type: Semisubterranean house
Principal Subsistence Type: Mix of animal and wild plant foods
Known informally as Pit River Indians, the Achumawi occupied regions of the Sierra Nevada foothills west of Mt Shasta. In his 1928 survey, Fred Kniffen noted a combined aboriginal population for Achumawi and Atsugewi of 3000 in 131 villages.

Acoma Pueblo (*see* Pueblo)

Agaiduka (*see* Shoshone)

Agua Caliente (*see* Cahuilla)

Aht (*see* Nootka)

Ahtena
Geographic Region: Subarctic (Canadian Northwest Territories)
Linguistic Group: Athapascan
Principal Dwelling Type: Double lean-to
Principal Subsistence Type: Caribou, moose

Akwaala
Geographic Region: Southwestern California (San Diego County)
Linguistic Group: Hokan-Yuman
Principal Dwelling type: Domed bark, thatch or hide house
Principal Subsistence Type: Acorns

Alabama (Alabamu)
Geographic Region: Southeast (Alabama)
Linguistic Group: Algonquian
Principal Dwelling Type: Rectangular thatched house
Principal Subsistence Type: Maize
The legends of the Alabama consider the tribe to have been one of the original tribes of the Southeast. They first came in contact with the white man in the person of Hernando De Soto in 1541, at which time they were living near the confluence of the Alabama and Tallapoosa rivers.

During the eighteenth century the Alabama were also encountered farther south in present-day Louisiana and Florida among the Caddo, Koasati and Seminole. Their language is identical to Koasati and similar to Choctaw and Chickasaw. They were described as industrious farmers, yet they were considered the fiercest warriors during the Creek War of 1813–14.

The Alabama were moved to Indian Territory in 1836, wherein their most important chief, Ward Coachman (1876–79), rose to prominence. The Alabama tribal government was considered to be a subdivision of the Creek government after 1906 and Alabama Town was given two seats on the Creek Tribal Council. The tribal population in 1730, according to French sources, was about 1600. The US government counted 321 Alabama Indians in 1833 prior to their removal to Oklahoma, and the 1950 census counted 500 in Oklahoma, Texas and Louisiana, an increase over the 192 counted in 1910.

Alachua (*see* Seminole)

Aleut
Geographic Region: Arctic (Aleutian Islands, Alaska)
Linguistic Group: Aleut
Principal Dwelling Type: Rectangloid earth-covered Alaskan house
Principal Subsistence Type:
    Sea mammals, fish, berries
    The Aleuts comprise two linguistic subgroups, the Unalaskans of the Alaskan

Above: **An 1875 photograph of an Abnaki man building a canoe in Houlton, Maine.** *Below:* **Aleut drying salmon in Alaska in 1887. The rectangular, earth-covered dwellings in the background were typical Aleutian structures. Traditionally, the Aleuts were excellent hunters and fishermen.**

Peninsula and the eastern Aleutian Islands; and the Atkans of the western Aleutian groups such as the Near, Rat and Andreanof islands. They are closely related to the nearby Eskimo, but are distinguished by their rounder faces. Traditionally they are good hunters and fishermen. At the time of their contact with Russian traders in 1741, they were estimated to number 20,000 or more. The

1910 US census showed only 1400, but by 1950 their number had increased to 5649. In 1985 the Aleutian Pribilof Island and Bristol Bay Native associations showed a combined population of 6369, but this did not account for those people living off the reservations.

Algonquian (*see* Abnaki, Arapahoe, Blackfoot, Cheyenne, Chippewa, Delaware, Fox, Kickapoo, Illinois, Mascouten, Massachuset, Mohegan, Narraganset, Ottawa, Potawatomi, Powhatan, Sauk, Wampanoag)
    The Algonquian Indians sharing the Algonquian language constitute North

American's largest group of tribes, with a population in excess of 250,000 in Canada and the United States. Their geographic range once spread from the Atlantic to the Rockies.

Alis

Geographic Region: Southeast (eastern Florida)
Linguistic Group:
  Muskogean-Alis (language extinct)
Principal Dwelling Type: Rectangular thatched house
Principal Subsistence Type: Fish, maize

Alsea

Geographic Region: Northwest (central Oregon coast)
Linguistic Group: Penutian
Principal Dwelling Type: Rectangular plank house
Principal Subsistence Type: Fish

Anadarko (Anadaca, Anadacao, Anadahcoe, Nadako)

Geographic Region: Plains (east Texas)
Linguistic Group: Caddoan
Principal Dwelling Type: Thatch or hide house
Principal Subsistence Type: Cultivated plants, game

The name Anadarko is Caddoan and means 'those who ate the honey of the bumble bee.' De Soto first made contact with these Indians in 1541 and called them Anondacao. They were included among the Caddo by early French surveys until 1763. Their numbers were reduced by conflict and disease, and in 1835 they were forced west to the Brazos River by the terms of the Caddo Treaty. In the Treaty of Council Springs (15 May 1846), the Anadarko, who numbered 450, agreed to accept the United States as their protector. In 1854 a reservation was set aside near Fort Belknap, Texas where there were said to be 202 Anadarko in 1857. In 1858 warfare broke out between the Anadarko and white settlers. As a result, they were moved to Indian Territory arriving on 1 August 1859, and settled on leased Choctaw lands in the Washita area. In 1861 the Civil War began, and Chief Jose Maria signed a treaty with the Confederate States of America, under whose auspices the tribe is said to have prospered. Attacks came from tribes sympathetic to the Union, forcing some Anadarko people north to Caddo country in Kansas until the end of the war. They returned to the Washita region in 1867 and have been associated with the Wichita-Caddo Reservation since 1901. In 1950 an estimated 449 Anadarko descendants remained

among the Caddo, and in 1985 the total Anadarko and Caddo population living at the Anadarko Agency in Oklahoma was 1218. *(see also* Caddo)

Anasazi

Geographic Region: Southwest
Linguistic Group: Uncertain
Principal Dwelling Type: Pueblo
Principal Subsistence Type: Mix of wild and cultivated plants

The Anasazi name means 'basket maker,' and is applied to a now extinct group of Indians who lived during prehistoric times in the four corners of the Southwest, where Arizona, New Mexico, Utah and Colorado meet. The Anasazi developed rudimentary basket making and agricultural techniques as early as 100 AD. They began making pottery around 500 AD, and began living in adobe houses

rather than caves about 700 AD. Between 1050 and 1300 the Anasazi culture reached its golden age, and elaborate cities filled with multistoried adobe buildings, such as Mesa Verde in Colorado, started to appear. Between 1300 and 1600, as their culture continued to flourish, streets and plazas became part of the city plans.

With the arrival of the Spanish, who conquered much of the Southwest, the Anasazi culture began to decline, and many of the cities were abandoned for more easily defended positions. The Anasazi also began to suffer raids by the Apache and Navajo during this period. Eventually factors such as disease, drought and intertribal warfare brought about the destruction of the Anasazi. It is possible that the remaining Anasazi became associated with the Pueblo tribes *(see also* Pueblo).

Left: The ruins of an Anasazi sandstone cliff dwelling, the White House, in Canyon de Chelly, Arizona. Many hundreds of Indians lived in this vast apartment complex and they became prosperous from farming the surrounding land. *Above:* This young Apache woman performs a traditional blessing with herb incense on the last remaining grounds of the aboriginal Pomos before the land is taken over by the construction of a California dam. The herbs are passed over the area being blessed. *Right:* Two Apache scouts and an Indian school boy sit for this 1884 photo in Wilcox, Arizona.

Apache

Geographic Region: Southwest (Arizona, Colorado, New Mexico, Oklahoma and Texas)

Linguistic Group: Athapascan (southern group)

Principal Dwelling Type: Crude conical tipi; domed bark, thatch or hide house

Principal Subsistence Type: Wild plants, small game

Subgroups: Aravaipa Apache, Chiricahua Apache, Cibecue Apache, Jicarilla Apache, Kiowa Apache, Lipan Apache, Mescalero Apache, Tonto Apache, Western Apache, White Mountain Apache

The major nomadic tribe in the American Southwest, the Apache, was also the last major tribe to surrender to government control in the 1880s. The name Apache derives from *apachu,* the Zuñi word for 'enemy.' The Apache call themselves N'de, Inde or Tinde, from the term *tinneh* meaning 'people.' The subgroup names include Chiricahua, 'mountain'; Jicarilla, 'little basket'; and Mescalero, 'mescal people.'

The Chiricahua once lived in Colorado and New Mexico in the Rio Grande drainage, and were first noted by Francisco Vasquez de Coronado in 1540. They were described as 'a gentle people, faithful in their friendships,' but by 1660 Spanish settlements were losing horses to Apache raiding parties. Prior to this time trade

had been carried out between the more nomadic Apache and the sedentary Pueblo peoples of Arizona and New Mexico. The Apache that lived in the Canadian River country of Texas and Oklahoma were frequently at war with the Comanche. In 1723 the Apache were defeated by the Comanche in a nine-day battle on the Wichita River, after which they moved farther south.

By 1736 the Apache were conducting guerrilla-style raids against neighbors on all sides—the Navajo to the west, the Spanish to the south and Comanche to the north. A peace treaty was signed at San Antonio, Texas on 19 August 1749. The people of San Antonio, constantly fearing Apache raiders, breathed freely, and Spanish missionary Father Santa Ana set out to convert the Apaches to Catholicism, with a decided lack of success.

The Kiowa Apache of the Colorado and Oklahoma plains were culturally and linguistically similar to the Apache groups of the Southwest, but they were politically

and geographically associated with the Kiowa and Pawnee. Meriwether Lewis and William Clark encountered them as far north as Wyoming. They were officially associated with the Kiowa on a Kiowa-Apache reservation by the terms of the Medicine Lodge Treaty of 1867.

The Lipan Apache call themselves Tcicihi, or 'people of the forest;' and were originally located on the plains of Texas and Oklahoma, farther east than any other Apache subgroup. They separated from the Jicarilla Apache in about 1600, and by 1700 they had sustained a long-standing feud with the Comanche. In 1846 they signed their first treaty with the US government, but became associated with the Confederate States of America during the Civil War. By 1885 the Tcicihi were peacefully settled in Indian Territory near Tonkawa, not far from the lands they had inhabited for the previous two centuries. In 1895 their band was merged with the Kiowa Apache.

On 1 July 1852 a treaty was signed at Santa Fe, New Mexico between the US government and the Apache of Arizona and New Mexico. However, the majority of the Chiricahua Apache who inhabited that region had little prior contact with the white man and could see little good coming from the treaty. Under their great Chief Mangus Colorado, the Apache continued the raids, which became particularly serious after 1858, when the Butterfield Overland Mail route began running its stagecoaches through Arizona and New Mexico.

Cochise, son-in-law of Mangus Colorado, was the second important Chiricahua Apache chief to have contact with the white man, and his relations with them were good from 1856 through to 1861. During that time, his band not only permitted the Butterfield Overland to operate through their territory, but they

openly supported it and helped establish a stage station at Apache Pass. In February 1861 Cochise was arrested at Apache Pass by the US Army for a kidnapping perpetrated by a rival band. He escaped but sought revenge on the Army by blocking the stage line. Wagon trains were attacked and miners driven out. Cochise and Mangus Colorado joined forces in opposition not only to the US Army but to the Army of the Confederacy that attempted to move into the Southwest from Texas during 1862.

The warfare was particularly bloody during 1862, with the Chiricahua Apache and Mescalero Apache successfully doing battle against the US Army, the Confederate Army and California Volunteers, who sought to hold the region against the Confederates. Mangus Colorado was taken prisoner while under a truce flag in January 1863, severely tortured and finally killed. Cochise and his 300 men continued the war against the whites until well after the conclusion of the Civil War. The raids were particularly fierce in 1870, forcing the US government to make serious peace overtures in 1871, after 10 years of warfare. When a band of Aravaipa Apache under Chief Eskiminzin attempted to surrender only to be massacred, peace seemed farther away than ever. Finally, in September 1872, General Oliver O Howard reached an accord with Cochise and the latter agreed to a ceasefire. The Chiricahua Apache remained at peace until after the death of Cochise in 1874.

When the US government decided to move the Chiricahua Apache out of their traditional lands in 1876, Taza, Cochise's son and heir, reluctantly agreed to the move. Some of the younger men who had grown up fighting alongside Cochise disagreed, however, and began the guerrilla war anew. Prominent among the leaders of the dissident factions were Naiche, Victorio and a man named Goyathlay, better known as Geronimo. Victorio was persuaded to join the Chiricahua reservation at San Carlos, but conditions there were so bad that he took to the hills with his band in September 1877. Two years later he had a band of 200 Chiricahua and Mescalero Apache and was making raids throughout the Southwest from a base in Mexico. But this time he had developed a reputation for savagery even among his followers. In a rare instance of cooperation, the US and Mexican governments agreed to work together to track him down. In October 1880 he was located and killed in a vicious battle with Mexican troops.

Left: **An Apache woman in traditional bridal costume.** *Above:* **Geronimo, one of Cochise's former lieutenants, conducted raids on white men after Cochise's death in 1874 until he was captured in 1886 and sent to Florida. Later, he was transferred to Fort Sill, Oklahoma, where he died in 1909.**

This left Geronimo as the principal warrior chief of the Apache. Pursued by US Army General George 'Grey Wolf' Crook, Geronimo followed Victorio's pattern, raiding the Southwest from a base in Mexico. Crook finally caught up with him in May 1883 and convinced him to surrender. From February 1884 to May 1885 Geronimo remained on the San Carlos reservation, during which time he was the subject of numerous newspaper articles recounting his deeds, both real and contrived by imaginative writers. When he left the reservation in May 1885, it was front page news on a national scale.

Crook located Geronimo in March 1886 and once again the Chiricahua were talked into a surrender. The short-lived surrender brought Crook's forced resignation and his replacement by General Nelson 'Bear Coat' Miles, who had made a name for himself during the Sioux and Nez Percé campaigns of the 1870s. Miles succeeded in capturing Geronimo for the

last time in August 1886. He and his Chiricahua band of 340 were sent to Fort Marion, Florida where many of them died. In October 1894 Geronimo and the remaining 296 men, women and children of his Chiricahua band were sent to Fort Sill, Oklahoma, a more agreeable climate for the southwestern Indians. Though he would technically remain a military prisoner of war for the rest of his life, Geronimo was considered harmless enough to be invited to ride in Theodore Roosevelt's inaugural parade in 1905 and in Pawnee Bill's Wild West Show in 1908. Geronimo died of pneumonia on 17 February 1909 in a small hut near the Fort Sill hospital at the age of 80. The Chiricahua Apache people at Fort Sill, including those born in Florida and Oklahoma after Geronimo's surrender, were considered prisoners of war until their official 'release' in 1913. In that year 87 of them were given land in Oklahoma.

In 1950 there were about 200 Chiricahua Apache, 30 Lipan Apache and 400 Kiowa Apache still living in Oklahoma out of an estimated total United States population of 8600 Apache, most of whom were living in the Southwest. In 1985 there were 2411 people at the Jicarilla Agency and Reservation in New Mexico, 2899 at the Mescalero Agency and Reservation in New Mexico, 8311 at the

Above: Nineteenth-century photos compare two important Indian dwelling types: the Apache's domed thatch and bark house (*left*) and the typical buffalo hide tipi of the Plains Indians as seen here in use by the Arapahoe. In the foreground, buffalo meat is drying on the poles. *Far left:* A Chiricahua Apache girl, granddaughter of Cochise, in an 1886 photo showing her dressed in traditional costume. *Left:* Chief Powder Face of the Arapahoe in war costume. The feathers on the headdress were rewards for achievement in battle and were cut or marked in a way that indicated the exact deed that earned them.

Fort Apache Agency and Reservation in Arizona, and 485 Apache at the Anadarko Agency in Oklahoma.

Apachicola, Apalachee (*see* Seminole)

Arapaho (Arapahoe)
Geographic Region: Plains and Prairies (eastern North Dakota and western Minnesota)
Linguistic Group: Uto-Aztecan
Principal Dwelling Type: Plains tipi
Principal Subsistence Type: Large game, buffalo

The name Arapaho is derived from the Pawnee *tirapihu (larapihu)* meaning 'he buys or trades,' an appropriate name for the greatest trading people of the Great Plains. They call themselves Invna-ina, or 'people of our own kind,' whereas their close allies the Cheyenne with whom they are historically allied, call them

Hitaniwo'iv, or 'cloud men.' Perhaps because of their historical inclination toward trading, they developed a reputation as friendly and a good deal less warlike than their friends the Cheyenne.

The oldest Arapaho legends place the tribe at the headwaters of the Mississippi near Lake Superior, from which they migrated west to the upper Missouri River country, where they first made contact with the Cheyenne. At about this time, the legends say that they 'lost the corn,' that is, they ceased to be planters and began to hunt buffalo. By 1835 large numbers of both the Arapaho and Cheyenne moved south into eastern Colorado while 'Northern' groups of the two tribes remained in Wyoming and Montana. The Southern Arapaho, under Chief Little Raven (Hosa), signed the Medicine Lodge Treaty in October 1867 with the US government by which the Arapaho agreed to live in peace on a reservation set aside for them in Oklahoma. After some confusion over the precise location of the reservation (the Red Fork of the Arkansas was misinterpreted as the Red River), the Arapaho Agency was established in 1870. An Arapaho School was opened the following year at Darlington, and it remained in operation until 1908, when it was merged with the Cheyenne Boarding School at Caddo Spring three miles away. The Arapaho steadfastly observed the Medicine Lodge Treaty and refused to join the Cheyenne, Comanche and Kiowa in the 1874–75 uprisings, despite extreme economic hardships during those years.

In 1890 the Arapaho, a historically religious people, became involved in the Ghost Dance religion that pledged the coming of a messiah who would unite all Indians living and dead. The Ghost Dance consisted of hypnotic rituals and dances, and had gained popularity among many Plains tribes, but by late 1890 the movement had dissipated for lack of the promised messiah. The Arapaho and Cheyenne sold 3,500,562 acres of their reservation lands to the US government in October 1890 for $1.5 million in return for 160 acres for each member of the tribes. When the land allotment was completed in 1892, the Arapaho population stood at 1091, down from 1664 in 1875 and the recorded peak of 2258 in 1881.

The Arapaho population continued to decline to 905 in 1902 and to the all-time reported low of 692 in 1924. There were 1189 Southern Arapahos on the Oklahoma reservation in Oklahoma in 1950, and in 1985 the Concho Agency (Cheyenne-Arapaho) showed a combined population of 5220.

Above: **A family group of the Bannock tribe in 1871, who lived in the Great Basin region of southern Idaho. Note the use of saplings in the construction of the tipi. This family is part of the sheep-eater group Bannock.**

Aravaipa Apache (*see* Apache)

Arikara (Arikaree)
Geographic Region: Plains and Prairies (Missouri River and along the border of North and South Dakota)
Linguistic Group: Caddoan
Principal Dwelling type: Prairie-Southeast earth lodge; domed bark, thatch or hide house
Principal Subsistence Type:
   Hunting, maize

The Arikara were associated with the Pawnee in Nebraska until the eighteenth century but moved north to the upper Missouri River country, where they settled near the Mandan and Hidatsa. They adapted to hunting buffalo, but were referred to in Plains Indian sign language as 'the corn eaters' because of their sedentary ways. When Lewis and Clark encountered them in 1804, the Arikara were estimated to have numbered 2600, but by 1950 the population was estimated at 500. In 1970 there were 1408 Arikara on reservations.

Arkansa Osage (*see* Osage)

Arosaguntacock (*see* Abnaki)

Assiniboin (Stoney)
Geographic Region: Plains and Prairies (western Saskatchewan)
Linguistic Group: Siouan
Principal Dwelling Type: Plains tipi
Principal Subsistence Type: Buffalo

The Assiniboin, whose name means 'one who cooks with stones,' were descendants of a group that split off from the Yanktonai Sioux in the seventeenth century. They were living near Lake Winnipeg in 1670 and later along the Assiniboin and Saskatchewan rivers in Canada. Along with Cree, they pushed the Black-

foot Indians out of western Saskatchewan. In the early nineteenth century they numbered roughly 800, but the smallpox epidemic of 1836 decimated half their population. They were later settled on reservations in Alberta and Montana, and in 1985 the Montana population stood at 2747.

Atakapa

Geographic Region: Southeast (Texas and Louisiana coast)
Linguistic Group: Algonquian
Principal Dwelling Type:
    Rectangular, thatched house
Principal Subsistence Type: Fish

Atasi (*see* Creek)

Atna

Geographic Region: Subarctic (Copper River Basin, southern Alaska)
Linguistic Group: Athapascan
Principal Dwelling Type: Rectangular, earth-covered Alaskan house

Principal Subsistence Type:
    Fish, caribou, moose

Atsina (*see* Gros Ventre)

Atsugewi

Geographic Region:
    Northeastern California (Pit River)
Linguistic Group: Hokan
Principal Dwelling Type:
    Semisubterranean house
Principal Subsistence Type: Mix of animal and wild plant foods

The Atsugewi were located in the northernmost regions of California along with the Achomawi and Modoc. In his 1928 survey, Fred Kniffen counted 131 Atsugewi and Achomawi villages with 3000 people.

Auk (*see* Tlingit)

Awatixa, Awaxawi (*see* Gros Ventre)

Ays (*see* Seminole)

Baffin Island Eskimo (*see* Eskimo)

Bannock

Geographic Region:
    Great Basin (southern Idaho)
Linguistic Group:
    Uto-Aztecan and Algonquian mix
Principal Dwelling Type: Crude conical tipi
Principal Subsistence Type: Large game

The Bannock constitute one of several numanic-speaking tribes, that is, they speak a language indigenous to the Great Basin. They are historically related to the

Shoshone, also of the rugged upper Great Basin country, where subsistence was difficult. In 1985 there were approximately 2250 Bannock on the Wind River Reservation in Wyoming.

Bear Lake (Satudene)

Geographic Region: Subarctic (Great Bear Lake, MacKenzie Territory)
Linguistic Group: Athapascan
Principal Dwelling Type: Double lean-to; crude conical tipi
Principal Subsistence Type:
  Fish, caribou, moose

The Bear Lake Indians are named for their proximity to the 12,000-square-mile Great Bear Lake located just north of the Arctic Circle in Canada's Northwest Territories. As part of the MacKenzie River drainage, the lake is close to the migrating range of the caribou, the centerpiece of the lifestyle of the Subarctic Indians.

Beaver

Geographic Region: Subarctic
Linguistic Group: Athapascan
Principal Dwelling Type: Double lean-to
Principal Subsistence Type:
Caribou, moose

In 1967, there were 727 Beaver Indians in Canada.

Bella Bella

Geographic Region:. Northwest Coast
Linguistic Group: Wakashan (related to Salishan)
Principal Dwelling Type:
  Rectangular plank house
Principal Subsistence Type: Fish

The Bella Bella are related to the Bella Coola and, like them, are located on the northern part of the British Columbia coast. The present town of Bella Bella is located near Campbell Island, British Columbia, about 150 miles south of Prince Rupert.

Bella Coola

Geographic Region: Northwest Coast
Linguistic Group: Salishan
Principal Dwelling Type:
  Rectangular plank house
Principal Subsistence Type: Fish

The Bella Coola, whose original home was on the Bella Coola River of the upper British Columbia coast, had a distinctive dialect owing to their isolation from other Salishan peoples. Though their language was similar to the Salishan-speaking people to the south, their culture was closer to that of the Kwakiutl. The Bella Coola first encountered the white man when Sir Alexander MacKenzie reached the Bella Coola River overland in July 1793. He noted that their homes were large cedar log buildings. He also observed their decorative and religious art, including their totem poles, carved to represent a 'totem' animal, an animal with which a particular family may be associated.

The present town of Bella Coola, British Columbia is located on a long inlet called Burke Channel, about 200 miles southeast of Prince Rupert and 50 miles east of Bella Bella, British Columbia. In 1967, there were 575 Bella Coola in Canada.

Beothuk

Geographic Region:
  Subarctic (Newfoundland only)
Linguistic Group: Beothukan

Below: A totem pole and gable-roofed house, capped by a thunderbird, the creator of thunderstorms, in a Bella Coola village in British Columbia, pre-1901. In the Northwest, houses were built by expert carpenters, and skilled craftsmen were hired to carve the totem poles for the front of the house. The totem poles were entirely secular, the equivalent of a European coat of arms. The height of the poles was limited only by the length of the great cedar log from which it was carved.

Principal Dwelling Type:
Crude conical tipi
Principal Subsistence Type:
Caribou, moose, sea mammals

The now extinct Beothuk originally inhabited the island we know as Newfoundland. They were encountered early in the European exploration of North America, and their habit of painting their bodies with red paint is thought to have led to the adoption of the term 'red man' to refer to Indians.

Biloxi

Geographic Region Southeast (southern Mississippi)
Linguistic Group: Muskogean
Principal Dwelling Type:
Rectangular thatched house
Principal Subsistence Type: Fish

The Biloxi were originally located on Biloxi Bay near the present site of Biloxi, Mississippi, but later they migrated toward Louisiana. They were originally thought to be related to the Choctaw who formed the majority of the population in the region, but in 1886 they were proven to be an isolated pocket of Siouan-speaking people. In 1985 the Tunica-Biloxi tribe in Louisiana had a population of 104.

Blackfoot (Siksika)

Geographic Region: Plains and Prairies (northern Montana and southern Alberta)
Linguistic Group: Algonquian
Principal Dwelling Type: Plains tipi
Principal Subsistence Type:
Large game, buffalo
Subgroups: Blackfoot Proper, Piegan Blackfoot, Blood Blackfoot

The Blackfoot are one of the several numanic-speaking tribes, and were historically allied with the nomadic Atsina. They were the archetypal Plains Indians, for whom the buffalo provided nearly all their needs, from food to clothing to leather for their tipis. When first encountered by the white man, they were located on the plains of Montana and Alberta immediately adjacent to the Rocky Mountains (which they called the 'backbone of the land'), but they were once thought to have lived as far east as the Great Lakes. The Blackfoot are among the westernmost of the Algonquian-speaking people. A traditional rivalry still exists among the three subgroups.

Right: **President Franklin Roosevelt shaking hands with Chief Bird Rattler of the Blackfoot tribe on 5 August 1934 in Glacier National Park, Montana after Chief Bird Rattler had inducted Roosevelt into his tribe, conferring upon him the title of 'Lone Chief.'**

Right: The Blackfoot depended upon the buffalo for nearly every facet of their existence. Charles M Russell portrayed the Indians in action in this 1919 painting. Hunting on horseback allowed the Plains Indian to move with great speed and agility. The hunter at right uses a rifle to down his quarry, but the bow and arrow was still a trusted weapon for killing buffalo.

Because of their dependence on buffalo, the Blackfoot were swift to adapt to the use of horses when they became available in the eighteenth century and soon they had large herds and a well-deserved reputation for horsemanship. When they obtained firearms, they became particularly potent raiders, attacking other tribes and the few whites who ventured into their remote lands. With horses and guns, the Blackfoot were masters of the North Plains: the buffalo were easier to hunt, and the other tribes feared the Blackfoot.

Beginning with the smallpox epidemic of 1836, however, the supremacy of the Blackfoot began to erode. By 1870 the tribe's population had been reduced by 66 percent over previous levels, and commercial hunting of the buffalo by white men was beginning to reduce the numbers of this once plentiful staple. By 1883 the buffalo were scarce to the point of verging on extinction and hard times had come. During the winter of 1883–84, called the 'starvation winter,' over 600 Blackfoot Indians died in Montana alone. Around the turn of the century, the traditional lifestyle of the Blackfoot was chronicled and preserved forever in the paintings of Montana artist Charles Russell, some of whose paintings are included here.

The Blackfoot had a highly developed religion with secret societies and mysticism in which medicine men, or shamans, were extremely important. Today Catholicism is the principal religion among the Blackfoot, although the traditional religion has not totally disappeared.

The present Blackfoot reservations are located in Alberta (where they numbered 7310 in 1967) and Montana on traditional Blackfoot lands. The principal Blackfoot city is Browning, Montana, which is also home to the Museum of the Plains Indian. In 1970 the population of the Montana reservation, which adjoins the eastern edge of Glacier National Park, was 5600, and in 1985 it was 6715. Some Blackfoot also live on the Fort Hall reservation in Idaho, and in excess of 5000 live off the reservations.

Blackfoot Sioux (*see* Sioux)

Blood Blackfoot (*see* Blackfoot)

Boise (*see* Shoshone)

Box Elder (*see* Shoshone)

Brandywine (*see* Wesort)

Brulé Sioux (*see* Sioux)

Buena Vista

Geographic Region: California (east central)
Linguistic Group: Penutian-Yokuts
Principal Dwelling Type: Crude conical tipi
Principal Subsistence Type: Acorns, small game

Bruneau (*see* Shoshone)

Bungi (*see* Chippewa)

Caddo

Geographic Region: Plains and Prairies (Texas)
Linguistic Group: Caddoan
Principal Dwelling type: Domed thatched house
Principal Subsistence Type: Maize

The Caddo, whose name drives from *kadohadacho,* meaning 'real chiefs,' are a traditionally prominent tribe in the Red and Arkansas river valleys of Oklahoma and Texas as well as parts of Louisiana and Arkansas, although they appear to have migrated from the Southwest in prehistoric times. The mounds discovered in the Arkansas drainage are thought to be of Caddo origin. De Soto encountered the Caddo in 1541, and by the time Sieur de La Salle visited them in 1686, they were

---

Opposite: **US Marine Corps reservists Minnie Spotted Wolf (***left***) of the Blackfoot tribe and Celia Mix of the Potawatomi tribe, photographed 16 October 1943.** *Below:* **The two C M Russell drawings at the bottom show the evolution of Blackfoot transportation. Prior to the arrival of the whites and the acquisition of horses, domesticated dogs pulled the travois. After the acquisition of horses, the dog was still part of Blackfoot life but no longer a beast of burden.**

associated with the Wichita and were a cornerstone of the regional confederacy. Their name for the region, Taches, was adapted by the early Spanish as Texas, a name which survives today.

From the time a French trading post was established at the Caddo city of Natchitoches in 1714, the tribe came under French influence. By the end of the eighteenth century the Caddo were at war with the Choctaw, who were being pushed west by the encroaching whites. In the early nineteenth century the Caddo became allied with the Choctaw against the Osage. In 1835 they sold their lands in Louisiana to the US government for $40,000 (in horses, other goods and cash annuities payable through 1840), and moved to the Washita River region of Oklahoma and the Brazos River region of Texas. In 1844 they were exempted from a Choctaw General Council ruling compelling non-Choctaw peoples to leave the Choctaw lands in southeastern Oklahoma.

On 15 May 1846, along with the related Anadarko people, the Caddo signed the Council Springs Treaty in which they acknowledged the US government as their protector and agreed to live in peace. They erected frame houses, engaged in agriculture and even supplied scouts for US Army actions against the Comanche. In August 1859, because of threats of attack by white Texans, the Caddo of Texas were moved north to Choctaw lands in the Washita River country where other Caddo were already living. The hurried departure of 1430 people and the two-week

In 1908, C M Russell painted *The Medicine Man*, which depicted a move across the plains by the Blackfoot tribe, a regular occurrence for the nomadic tribes as they followed the buffalo. Women, children and elders traveled in the middle of the party while guards remained at the rear to protect against enemy attack. Each family was responsible for its own belongings, which they hauled by travois or on their backs. Even with the horse, progress was slow, around five miles being covered each day. The medicine man was second only to the chief in his importance to the group. His duties involved both religious interpretation and pharmacology. A good medicine man became adept at both and as a result he was often thought of as possessing magical powers.

Above: **A detail of a painting by George Catlin which shows La Salle's greeting by the Caddo.** *Right:* **A Cayuse brave.**

march in the August heat proved a severe hardship, and the Caddo were still pursued by the Texans. On 12 August 1861 Chief Quinahiwi, together with leaders of other tribes, signed a treaty with the Confederate States of America, and some Caddo people went on to serve with the Confederacy during the Civil War. The latter took part in the destruction of the Wichita Agency in 1862 and the massacre of the Tonkawa. The Confederate Army's Caddo Battalion was among the last to surrender in July 1865.

By 1867 the Caddo were resettled in the Washita region where they established homes and farms, and in 1872 a Wichita-Caddo reservation was established. A new tribal organization was formed, and its corporate charter was approved in 1936. On 17 January 1938 the bylaws were ratified, replacing the tribal chief with a tribal council. Enoch Hoag earned the distinction of being the last Caddo chief.

The Caddo population was estimated at about 800 in 1805, and it roughly doubled by the time the Texas and Oklahoma branches of the Washita Caddo consolidated in 1859. By 1880, there were estimated to be 538 Caddo, and by 1897 the number had declined to 497. The 1930 census showed a population of 1005, and a government survey of 1944 showed 1165. In 1985 the total population of Caddo and Anadarko living at the Anadarko Agency in Oklahoma was 1218. *(See also Anadarko)*

Cahokia

Geographic Region: Northeast (Illinois)
Linguistic Group: Algonquian
Principal Dwelling Type: Domed bark, thatch or hide house
Principal Subsistence Type: Hunting, maize

The Cahokia were prominent among the prehistoric mound builders of the upper Mississippi River country. The

Cahokia Mound in Madison County, Illinois near St Louis is the largest prehistoric earthwork in North America. The Cahokia are traditionally associated with the Tamaroa, and the two were first encountered by Jesuit missionaries near present-day Cahokia, Illinois in 1698. The Cahokia formed a confederation with the Illinois, Kaskaskia and Peoria; in 1818, the confederacy ceded half the present state of Illinois to the United States and became part of the Kaskaskia and Peoria tribes.

Cahuilla

Geographic Region: Southwest (Palm Springs, southeastern California)
Linguistic Group: Uto-Aztecan
Principal Dwelling Type: Domed bark, thatch or hide house
Principal Subsistence Type: Wild plants, maize, small game

Although known as one of the 'mission peoples' tribes, the Cahuilla were the principal desert tribe of southern California not to have been associated with the early Spanish missions. With a few exceptions, the Cahuilla did not become 'mission Indians.' The missions encouraged intermarriage, which blurred distinctions between tribes, but the Cahuilla did not begin to intermarry until the latter part of the nineteenth century. Alfred Kroeber estimated in 1925 that the aboriginal Cahuilla population had been roughly 2500. In 1970 there were 354 Cahuilla on seven Southern California reservations, including 23 on the Cahuilla Reservation itself. In 1985 the population of the Cahuilla Reservation was 148.

Calapooya (*see* Kalapuya)

Calusa

Geographic Region: Southeast (southwestern Florida)
Linguistic Group: Muskogean
Principal Dwelling Type: Rectangular thatched house
Principal Subsistence Type: Fish

Capaha (*see* Quapaw)

Caribou Eskimo (*see* Eskimo)

Carrier

Geographic Region: Subarctic (coastal mountains, Alaska and British Columbia)
Linguistic Group: Athapascan
Principal Dwelling Type: Crude conical tipi, double lean-to
Principal Subsistence Type: Caribou, moose

The Carrier, like other Subarctic tribes of British Columbia, were nomadic peoples who followed the caribou as their principal source of subsistence. Their basketry consisted only of coiling, which distinguished Indians of this region from those of the Northwest Coast or Alaska, where a combination of coiling and twining were used.

In 1967, there were 3862 Carrier in Canada.

Cascade

Geographic Region: Great Basin (Columbia River, north central Oregon)
Linguistic Group: Penutian-Chinook
Principal Dwelling Type: Semisubterranean house
Principal Subsistence Type: Fish

Catawba

Geographic Region: Southeast (southern South Carolina)
Linguistic Group: Siouan
Principal Dwelling type: Rectangular barrel-roofed house
Principal Subsistence Type: Maize

The Catawba, whose name is derived from the Yuchi word *Kotaba,* or 'strong people,' were the prominent Siouian-speaking tribe in the Southeast. Catawba legend indicates that they migrated into South Carolina from the northwest, where they had lived as farmers and hunters. When first encountered by the Spanish in 1566, they were still referring to themselves by their traditional name Iswa, or Ysa.

There had been a good deal of warfare between the Catawba and their longstanding rivals, the Shawnee and the Iroquois. The great Catawba Chief Haiglar was murdered by the Shawnee on 30 August 1763. Relations between the Catawba and

white people had been good, and Chief Haiglar had even helped the whites defeat the Cherokee in 1759. During the American Revolution, the Catawba joined the Americans against the British. At its peak in the postwar period (1822), the Catawba population measured 450. In 1840 the tribe sold the major part of its land and attempted unsuccessfully to live in North Carolina. In 1848, having returned to South Carolina, they petitioned the US government for the right to move to Indian Territory. In 1853 the Choctaw Nation of Indian Territory granted the Catawba the right to settle on their land and become Choctaws. Some Catawba moved to Indian Territory to join the Creek and Choctaw, but the main portion of the tribe remained in York County, South Carolina, their homeland, where some Catawbas served with the Confederate Army during the Civil War. In 1944 all 300 members of the tribe were granted the rights and privileges of citizens of South Carolina.

Cayuga (*see* Iroquois)

Cayuse

Geographic Region: Great Basin (northeastern Oregon)
Linguistic Group: Klamath-Sahaptin
Principal Dwelling Type: Crude conical tipi
Principal Subsistence Type: Mix of animal and wild plant foods

Celilo

Geographic Region: Great Basin (eastern Oregon along Columbia River)
Linguistic Group: Penutian-Sahaptin
Principal Dwelling Type: Crude conical tipi
Principal Subsistence Type: Mix of animal and wild plant foods

Chasta-Costa

Geographic Region: Northwest Coast (central Oregon coast)
Linguistic Group: Athapascan
Principal Dwelling type: Rectangular plank house
Principal Subsistence Type: Fish

The 1970 population of the Chasta-Costa was 30.

Chaui (*see* Pawnee)

Chehalis

Geographic Region: Northwest Coast (western Washington)
Linguistic Group: Salishan
Principal Dwelling Type: Rectangular plank house

Left: **A Cherokee elder heats a stone axehead over a fire at the Cherokee reservation in North Carolina.** *Above:* **Cherokee weaving baskets at Tsa-La-Gi Indian village near Tahlequah, Oklahoma. Tahlequah was the capital of the Cherokee Nation until the latter was officially disbanded on 14 June 1914.**

Principal Subsistence Type: Fish

The Chehalis reservation, located on Washington's Olympic Peninsula, had a population of 777 in 1985. The tribe includes descendants of those members of the Chinook tribe who joined the Chehalis and adopted their language after an epidemic in 1829.

Chelan

Geographic Region: Northwest Coast (north-central Washington)
Linguistic Group: Salishan
Principal Dwelling Type: Rectangular plank house
Principal Subsistence Type: Fish

Chemakum

Geographic Region: Northwest Coast (Puget Sound, Washington)
Linguistic Group: Salishan
Principal Dwelling Type: Rectangular plank house
Principal Subsistence Type: Fish

Chemehuevi (Southern Paiute, *see* Paiute)

Cherokee

Geographic Region: Southeast (Carolinas, Georgia, Tennessee)
Linguistic Group: Iroquoian
Principal Dwelling Type: Rectangular thatched house
Principal Subsistence Type: Hunting, maize

The Cherokee were one of the largest tribes in the Southeast and were among the earliest to adapt to European civilization. Their name is written Tsálagi in their own language, and they were called Chalakki by the Choctaw, whose language was the language of trade in the Southeast.

When De Soto made contact with them in 1540, the Cherokee had developed a very complex culture and society in the region surrounding their capital city, Echota (Itsati), near the present site of Madisonville, Tennessee. In the seventeenth century their capital was moved to New Echota (Ustanali) near present-day Calhoun, Georgia. In 1729 an estimated 20,000 Cherokee were living in 64 towns and villages.

Even as European civilization was gaining a foothold on North America's Atlantic coast, the Cherokee were expanding their own empire to the west. They defeated the Tuscarora of the Carolinas in 1711, drove the Shawnee out of the Cumberland River country in 1715 and later contributed to the breakup of the Catawba. Their 1755 defeat of the Creek in the Battle of the Taliwa was a turning point in the struggle for control of the northern Georgia country. Subsequent warfare with the British ended in Chief Attakullakulla's peace treaty, signed in Charleston in 1761.

After their defeat by the Chickasaw in 1768, the influence of the once powerful Cherokee began to decline. After a series of wars and the loss of considerable territory to white settlers, Chief Dragging Canoe (son of Attakullakulla) concluded the treaty of 1777 and moved a portion of the Cherokee tribe to Chickamauga Creek near Chattanooga, Tennessee. After taking the name Chickamauga, the western Cherokee began a series of wars with the whites that continued until the Cherokee removal in 1839 to Indian Territory.

The eastern Cherokee, meanwhile, became successful farmers and developed an advanced municipal structure in their towns and villages. They built large houses and owned large herds of cattle. They went so far in their emulation of white plantation owners that some prominent Cherokee even acquired Negros as slaves.

In 1808 Chief Charles Hicks set down the Cherokee legal code in written form. At the same time, Sequoia (Sequoya), a Cherokee from Alabama, was in the process of developing what was to be the first written (nonpictorial) language to originate in North America. He developed an 85 character alphabet that contained every inflection needed to write the Cherokee language, and by 1822 many Cherokee were reading and writing in their own language. Sequoia's alphabet was cast in metal type, and books and periodicals were published. The bilingual (Cherokee-English) *Cherokee-Phoenix* was first published at New Echota on 21 February 1828.

With a population of about 13,000, the Cherokee Nation under Chief John Ross was a force to be reckoned with, and in 1828 Georgia placed it under state jurisdiction. The Cherokees sued the state in the US Supreme Court and lost. In May 1836 a treaty was ratified by the US Senate that called for the Cherokee to give up their lands in Georgia in exchange for new lands in Indian Territory, effective in May 1838. Some Cherokee were removed peacefully and some by force. Of those who made the 800-mile trek during the winter of 1838–39, over 4000 died.

On 12 July 1839 the eastern and western Cherokee merged as 'one body politic, under the style and title of the Cherokee Nation.' The nation was established in the northeast corner of Indian Territory, and on 6 September 1839 a constitution was adopted. A public school system was established in 1841. Two years later 18 schools were in operation, and by 1851 there were two 'seminaries' of higher learning. A Cherokee printing house was established in 1844 and began publication of the *Cherokee Advocate,* a bilingual newspaper utilizing Sequoia's alphabet.

With the start of the Civil War in 1861, the Cherokee, under Chief John Ross, became allied with the Confederate States of America and a Cherokee regiment was organized. The commander of this regiment, Stand Watie, reached the rank of brigadier general in the Confederate Army.

The business of the Cherokee Nation resumed after the war, but by 1889 white settlement of nearby 'Oklahoma country' brought pressure on the Indians to sell their lands to whites. On 7 August 1902 Chief T M Buffington called a special

election in which the Cherokee people chose to each take 110 acres of land from the Cherokee Nation. In March 1907 the Cherokee Nation ceased to exist, and on 30 June 1914 the Cherokee national government officially went out of business, although Chief William Rogers remained in office through 1917 to sign deeds.

The Cherokee population, like that of most tribes, fluctuated dramatically in the nineteenth century. In 1808, when Chief Hicks first set down the Cherokee legal code, there were 12,395 eastern Cherokee living in the towns of the east, plus roughly 2000 western Cherokee in Tennessee. In 1835, prior to their removal to Indian Territory, there were 16,542 eastern Cherokee in the east (of which nearly 25 percent perished in the journey), and about 6000 western Cherokee in Indian Territory. By the Civil War, the combined Cherokee Nation was said to have had a population of 21,000, but in 1867 the number had dwindled to 13,566.

In the twentieth century, the population in Oklahoma (former Indian Territory) increased from 41,693 at the time of dissolution of the Cherokee Nation government in 1914 to 45,238 in 1930. Over the next half century many Cherokee left Oklahoma, so that by 1982 the Cherokee tribe at the Tahlequah Agency in Oklahoma numbered only 42,992. In North Carolina the descendants of those Cherokee who returned to the East numbered 6110 at the Cherokee Agency and Reservation.

Chewelah
Geographic Region: Great Basin (eastern Washington)
Linguistic Group: Salishan

Left: A Cherokee boy and girl in traditional costume on a North Carolina reservation. *Above:* Lt Woody J Cochran, a Cherokee from Oklahoma, was a bomber pilot who earned the Siver Star, Purple Heart, Distinguished Flying Cross, and the Air Medal for his actions and bravery during World War II. *Facing page:* Cheyenne tribe members Dull Knife (*left*) and Little Wolf, who were instrumental in establishing a reservation for the Northern Cheyenne.

Principal Dwelling Type:
 Semisubterranean house
Principal Subsistence Type: Fish, game
Note: Subgroup of Spokane tribes

Cheyenne
Geographic Region: Plains and Prairies (Black Hills area, South Dakota and areas in neighboring states)
Linguistic Group: Algonquian
Principal Dwelling type: Plains tipi
Principal Subsistence Type: Buffalo

The Cheyenne were one of the major Plains tribes, traditionally allied with the Arapaho and at odds with the Sioux. When first encountered by La Salle in 1680, they were living in present-day Minnesota, but later they migrated to the Cheyenne River in present-day North Dakota, a region that the Sioux named 'the place where the Cheyenne plant.' That name indicates that they once pursued agriculture. Eventually, as legend tells it, they 'lost the corn' and evolved into buffalo hunters like most of the other Plains tribes.

By the time they met Lewis and Clark in 1804, the Cheyenne were in the Black Hills area of South Dakota, having been pushed off the plains by the Sioux. In 1851 some of the tribe moved south to the Arkansas River country, becoming known as the Southern Cheyenne and at the same time becoming associated with the southern wing of the Arapaho tribe. By terms of the 1867 Medicine Lodge Treaty, the

US government assigned a joint reservation to the Southern Arapaho and Southern Cheyenne.

Prior to this, Cheyenne relations with whites had been reasonably good despite the 'Sand Creek Massacre,' an 1864 unprovoked, surprise attack by the US Army Cavalry under Colonel J M Chivington on the Cheyenne encampment under Chief Black Kettle. In 1868, however, the Cheyenne did take part in a major Plains Indian war. During this war on 27 November, Chief Black Kettle's camp, this time on the Washita River in Oklahoma, was again the subject of a surprise attack by the US Army. The attacking force was the Army's seventh Cavalry under Colonel George Armstrong Custer.

The attack resulted in the death of Chief Black Kettle and many years of animosity between the Cheyenne and the whites, which lasted until 1875. The Washita battle also served to promote and enhance the career and popularity of the flamboyant Custer.

Meanwhile, in the Dakota country to the north, the Northern Cheyenne had long since made peace with their traditional rivals, the Sioux. They participated in numerous joint attacks against the whites of the northern plains during the 1860s and 1870s. It was in the summer of 1876 that the US Army made a concentrated effort to track down the Indians, defeat them in battle and send them back to their reservations. In late June of that

year a major encampment was underway on the banks of the Little Bighorn River in southeastern Montana. There were several thousand Indians present, making it one of the largest Indian encampments ever to take place in North America. Most of those present were Sioux, but a large band of Northern Cheyenne, under Chief Crazy Horse, were present as a guest tribe. Several columns of seventh Cavalry were also in the area, and on the morning of 15 June one of these, commanded by Colonel Custer, attacked the enormous gathering. Though greatly outnumbered, Custer was hoping for a repeat of his success on the Washita. The attack proved to be a gross miscalculation and Custer's entire force was killed in the most re-

sounding defeat that the US Army would suffer in the Indian Wars.

The tribal groups that had been together coincidentally on the Little Big-horn went their separate ways, and a greatly reinforced US Army was able to force the smaller groups into submission and onto the Indian Territory reservation by 1877. The Northern Cheyenne were not used to conditions in the south and many became ill. In September 1878 Chiefs Little Wolf and Dull Knife decided to take 353 of their followers back to the north, and they slipped off the reservation. Some of their group were captured enroute, but most were able to get through to Montana, where they convinced the US government to allow them to stay. A

Below: A late nineteenth-century photograph of a Cheyenne camp showing a wagon and a canvas-covered tipi — by-products of the white man's contribution to their lifestyle. Meat and sausage are seen drying on the racks in the traditional way.

Northern Cheyenne reservation was established on Montana's Tongue River, and in 1883 all the Northern Cheyenne were resettled there from Indian Territory.

In 1885 the population of the Northern Cheyenne Agency and Reservation in Montana was 3177, up from 2100 in 1970. The Cheyenne-Arapaho Reservation in Oklahoma had 6674 people in 1970 and 5220 in 1985.

Chiaha (*see* Seminole)

Chickahominy
Geographic Region: Northeast
Linguistic Group: Algonquian
Principal Dwelling Type: Rectangular barrel-roofed house
Principal Subsistence Type: Maize

Chickamauga (*see* Cherokee)

Chickasaw
Geographic Region: Southeast (Mississippi)
Linguistic Group: Muskogean
Principal Dwelling Type: Rectangular thatched house
Principal Subsistence Type: Maize
The Chickasaw were once part of the

Choctaw tribe whose language is virtually identical, and their name means 'they left as a tribe not a very great while ago.' When encountered by De Soto in 1540, they were living in present-day Mississippi, although their legends speak of their having migrated from the west. As De Soto discovered first hand, they had a reputation as skilled warriors. Their record of victories during the eighteenth century is exemplary of the skill that made them a leading military force in the lower Mississippi valley: they defeated the Shawnee in 1715 and 1745, the Caddo in 1717, the Cherokee in 1768 and the Creek in 1795.

Despite their hostility to other tribes, the Chickasaw traded extensively with the English throughout the eighteenth century and signed a treaty with the newly formed United States in 1786. In 1837 the US government decided to remove the Chickasaw to Indian Territory, where an agreement had been reached to settle them on Choctaw lands and to give them Choctaw citizenship. In 1855 a new arrangement was made granting them their own land within Indian Territory, on land formerly part of the Choctaw Nation. The capital of this new Chickasaw Nation was named in

honor of the late great Chickasaw chief, Tishomingo, who had died on the journey west in 1838 at the age of 102.

The governments of the two nations were suspended during the Civil War and re-established in 1866. The governments of all the Indian Territory tribes were dissolved in 1906 prior to the entry of Indian Territory into the United States as part of Oklahoma. The Chickasaw Tribal Protective Association was formed in 1929.

The population of the Chickasaw tribe was 2290 in 1780, down from an estimated 3300 at the beginning of the eighteenth century. In 1890 there were 6400 Chickasaw, and 5350 still lived on the Chickasaw reservation in Oklahoma in 1944. In 1985 the Ardmore Agency of the Chickasaw tribe in Oklahoma had a population of 9020.

Chilkat (*see* Tlingit)

Chilocotin
Geographic Region: Subarctic (coastal mountains, Alaska and British Columbia)
Linguistic Group: Athapascan
Principal Dwelling type: Rectangular plank house, double lean-to

Left: Cheyenne Indians, dressed in historical costume, demonstrate the use of the travois, the traditional equipment for transporting supplies, food and children, at the 1951 Cheyenne pageant in Rapid City, South Dakota. *Above:* These Cheyenne Indians in this 1887 photograph prepare to skin a deer.

Principal Subsistence Type: Fish, caribou, moose

Chimakuan

Geographic Region: Northwest Coast (western Washington)
Linguistic Group: Mosan (Wakashan-Salish, dialect extinct)
Principal Dwelling Type: Rectangular plank house
Principal Subsistence Type: Fish

Chinook

Geographic Region: Northwest Coast (Oregon and Washington coast)
Linguistic Group: Penutian-Chinook
Principal Dwelling Type: Rectangular plank house
Principal Subsistence Type: Fish, game
Subgroups:
Clatsop (northern Oregon coast)
Kathlamet (northern Oregon coast)
Wahkiakum (southern Washington coast)

The traditional homeland of the Chinook people was the area around the mouth of the Columbia River and spreading north and south on the Oregon and Washington coast. The mainstay of their livelihood and primary food source was the salmon that swam upstream in the Columbia every year to spawn. One variety of salmon, the King Salmon *(Oncorhynchus tschawytscha),* is commonly known as the Chinook Salmon. The Chinook diet was supplemented with other seafood such as the crabs and clams common to the North Pacific coast, as well as deer and elk from the nearby woods.

The first contact the Chinook had with the white man was with the explorer John Meares, who arrived at Willapa Bay in 1788. The Chinook met his ship in large, brightly painted, cedar log canoes and introduced him to their complex and highly developed culture. When Lewis and Clark reached the mouth of the Columbia in 1805, the Chinook numbered about 400, but an epidemic in 1829 destroyed over half the tribe. Many of the surviving Chinook joined the nearby Salishan-speaking Chehalis tribe and adopted their language.

In 1885 John Wesley Powell's survey found more than 500 Chinook living on the coast and on the Grand Ronde, Warm Springs and Yakima Reservations in central Washington and Oregon.

Chipewyan

Geographic Region: Subarctic (Great Slave Lake, MacKenzie Territory)
Linguistic Group: Athapascan
Principal Dwelling Type: Crude conical tipi
Principal Subsistence Type: Fish, caribou, moose

The Chipewyan were the major tribe of the central subarctic region of North America west of Hudson Bay. They had a good deal of contact with the Eskimo to the north and the Cree to the south, as well as the other Subarctic tribes to the north west. Trading was important to the Chipewyan and their location made them the region's keystone. The caribou was their staple food source, but other supplementary sources were available such as moose, musk oxen and Canada geese.

The first white men to contact the Chipewyan were traders from the Hudson Bay Company who arrived in 1717. The Chipewyan soon included the white men

Above: Based on the journal writings of Lewis and Clark, Charles Russell painted their encounter with Chinook Indians in 1805 on the lower Columbia River. The Shoshone woman, Sacagawea, served as guide and interpreter of sign language for the two explorers as they carried out their peaceful mission. This meeting was one of the first encounters between the Northwest tribes and the white man. The elaborately carved canoes of the Chinooks were constructed without nails or metal parts of any kind, yet they rivaled those of Lewis and Clark in both size and sophistication.

among their trading partners and eagerly traded furs and hides for European wares such as clothing and guns. In 1717 the tribe was said to have numbered about 3500, but a smallpox epidemic reduced their number to below 500. During the nineteenth century their number gradually increased so that by 1906 there were 2400 Chipewyan. In the twentieth century the Chipewyan benefited from increased Canadian government services such as schools. By 1970 there were 4643 Chipewyan living in 16 settlements in Canada's Northwest Territories.

Chippewa (Ojibwa)

Geographic Region: Northeast (Canadian Shield: Quebec, Ontario, Minnesota, Michigan and surrounding areas)
Linguistic Group: Algonquian

Principal Dwelling type: Domed bark, thatch or hide house
Principal Subsistence Type: Game, fish, wild rice
Subgroups: Northern Ojibwa in Manitoba and Ontario Bungi (Salteaux), a western offshoot in Manitoba and Saskatchewan

The Chippewa were the largest and most powerful tribe in the Great Lakes country, with a range that extended from the edge of Iroquois territory in the Northeast to the Sioux-dominated Great Plains. Both of these major tribes were traditional Chippewa rivals, but neither was powerful enough to threaten the Chippewa heartland, where the Chippewa was master. The tribe used the lakes and rivers of the region like a vast highway network, and developed the birch bark

Above: **Chippewa hunters in birch-bark canoe around 1900. The Chippewa tribesmen were expert hunters who used the birch-bark canoe and the many rivers of the north central region to form a vast transportaion network.** *Right:* **A Chippewa woman harvesting wild rice in Minnesota around 1925. Ten days before the rice was ripe, a woman established a claim to a portion of the crop by tying portions of it into small sheaves.** *Far right:* **A Chippewa encampment with bark-covered wigwams near Red River, Canada in 1858.** *Overleaf:* **A George Catlin drawing (c 1840) of the Chippewa historical costumes and facial features.**

canoe into one of the continent's major means of transportation.

By the time they made contact with the white man in the early seventeenth century, the Chippewa probably numbered 35,000 and constituted the largest single tribe north of Mexico. In the face of white encroachment they formed alliances with other tribes against intruders. They joined

Pontiac's Ottawa in the 1763 attack on Detroit, and later allied themselves with Tecumseh and the Shawnee in the series of Indian wars that immediately preceded the War of 1812. They continued the battle against white domination throughout most of the nineteenth century, despite the US government's efforts to organize them onto reservations. The last battle between the US Army and the Chippewa came at Leach Lake, Minnesota in 1898.

In 1967 there were 43,948 Chippewa in Canada. In 1985 there were 17,247 Chippewa on reservations in Minnesota, 9583 in North Dakota and 8138 in Wisconsin.

Chiricahua Apache (*see* Apache)

Chitimacha
Geographic Region:
  Southeast (Mississippi Delta)
Linguistic Group:
  Muskogean-Chitimacha
Principal Dwelling Type: Rectangular
  thatched house
Principal Subsistence Type: Fish

The Chitimacha, who lived at the mouth of the Mississippi River, were particularly noted for their dried cane basketry, which was woven by a technique known as twilled plaiting. The warp and weft were identical in size and the result was a very angular design. Black and red vegetable dyes were made from walnut and oak bark, respectively, and were used to accent the natural yellow or green of the dried cane.

The initiation rites of the Chitimacha included sealing the youths in a ceremonial house for six days of fasting and ritual dance. In his 1911 survey, John Swanton noted that the Chitimacha had a very carefully arranged and firmly enforced caste system similar to that of the Natchez. In the caste system positions were inherited through one's mother, except for the role of chief, which was passed on from father to son. The castes included the nobility (which in turn included the Suns, Nobles and Honored People), and the commoners, who were called Stinkards.

In 1982 the population of the Chitimacha Reservation in Louisiana numbered 325 persons, up from 270 in 1970.

Choctaw (Chahta)
Geographic Region:
  Southeast (Mississippi)
Linguistic Group: Algonquian
Principal Dwelling Type: Rectangular
  thatched house
Principal Subsistence Type: Maize, fish
The Choctaw, whose original name

okla homa means 'red people,' originated in the lower Mississippi and were once related to Chickasaw of the same region. The tribal legends tell of a *nanih waya* ('productive mountain') built by a great red man who then created the red people. Nanih Waya is thought to be a mound that was located in Winston County, Mississippi, the site of the last, great national council of the Choctaw in 1828.

The Choctaw first came across the white man when they were attacked by De Soto on 18 October 1540. There was little further contact until the eighteenth century, by which time the population of the tribe numbered as many as 20,000 in 115 villages. In the early eighteenth century they became allied with the French against the English, the Chickasaw and the Natchez. By 1736, however, a pro-English faction had developed within the tribe. After the British defeat of the French in

1763, a treaty was signed in 1765 between the English and the Choctaw, although the latter remained largely sympathetic to the French. The tribe supported the Americans during the Revolutionary War, and in 1786 signed their first treaty with the United States at Hopewell, South Carolina.

After 1820, the pressure for the removal of all Indians to west of the Mississippi led to the Choctaw being assigned lands in present-day Oklahoma, where some Choctaw hunters already had gone in search of game. A treaty providing for the final removal of the entire Choctaw Nation was signed at Dancing Rabbit Creek, Mississippi on 28 September 1830. In the treaty, the Choctaw traded their Mississippi lands for the new lands, which constituted the entire southern swath of the region that would come to be known as Indian Territory. The constitution of the new

Choctaw Nation was adopted on 3 June 1834.

In 1837 the Choctaw granted the Chickasaw the right to settle within the Choctaw Nation, and in 1855 a portion of the Choctaw Nation was set aside for the formation of a Chickasaw Nation. During the Civil War, both nations allied themselves with the Confederate States of America, and formed military units that fought with the Confederacy in Arkansas and Indian Territory. At the time of the postwar re-establishment of the two nations in 1866, an idea evolved for a merger of all the tribal governments within Indian Territory into a single Indian government. It was a Choctaw delegate, Allen Wright, who suggested the name 'Oklahoma' for such a territory. In 1890 a territory *was* formed out of part of Indian Territory and named Oklahoma, and in 1907 all of the Indian Territory and Okla-

homa territory lands joined the United States as the state of Oklahoma. With the establishment of the state in 1907, tribal government was largely dissolved, although the offices of principal chief, national attorney and mining trustee were retained until 1948. The present system of a Choctaw Tribal Council retains the office of principal chief.

By the terms of the Indian Reorganization Act of 1934, the Choctaw Tribal Council was officially established in Mississippi to represent the Choctaw that remained in the traditional Choctaw homeland adjacent to the historic Nanih Waya mound. A constitution was passed in April 1945, and in 1973 the Bureau of Indian Affairs was persuaded to name a Choctaw as head of its Choctaw Agency in Mississippi. The mid-summer Choctaw Fair is an important social event for the Mississippi band of the Choctaw and in-

Above: **A Choctaw Indian demonstrating the use of the cane blowgun around 1909. The Choctaw used the blowguns to hunt squirrels, rabbits and birds. Cane blowguns were unique to the tribes of the Southeast. The kill was accomplished by shooting a poison dart through the blowgun at close range.**

cludes the tribal championship in Choctaw stickball, a game which had been a tradition among Choctaw since prehistoric times.

In Mississippi most Choctaw are bilingual and 90 percent of Choctaw homes use the native tongue as their primary language.

In 1831, prior to their removal to Indian Territory, the Choctaw population in Mississippi was 19,554. At the close of the removal in 1837 there were 12,500 in the new Choctaw Nation, with 2500 recorded to have died enroute to the new lands. In 1904 there were 17,775 Choctaw in Indian Territory (soon to become the state of

Oklahoma), including 2225 who had arrived from Mississippi after the Civil War. In 1944 there were 19,000 Choctaw in Oklahoma and 2232 in Mississippi. In 1985 the Talihina Agency of the Choctaw Tribe in Oklahoma had a population of 20,054 and the Choctaw Agency in Mississippi had a population of 4599.

Choushatta (*see* Koasati)

Choya'ha (*see* Yuchi)

Chukchansi
Geographic Region: California (east central)
Linguistic Group: Penutian-Yokuts
Principal Dwelling type: Crude conical tipi
Principal Subsistence Type: Acorns, small game
The reservation at Table Mountain, California had a population of 88 in 1985.

Chumash
Geographic Region: California (Santa Barbara)
Linguistic Group: Hokan
Principal Dwelling Type: Domed bark, thatch or hide house

Principal Subsistence Type: Acorns, fish
The traditional home of these noted ocean fishermen was on the mainland and islands of the south-central California coast, from the areas adjacent to the Spanish missions of (and later California counties) San Luis Obispo and Santa Barbara, south along the Santa Barbara Channel to present-day Los Angeles.
Estimates of Chumash population prior to Spanish contact range from 13,650 to 20,400. The Chumash were organized into between 107 to 136 villages on the mainland and Santa Barbara Channel islands. Spanish mission records indicate that as many as 4935 Indians were baptized as Catholics in the 38 largest villages prior to 1771. The Chumash people, like many California Indians, were almost completely integrated into Spanish mission society prior to California's becoming part of the United States. In 1985 the population of the Santa Ynez Reservation near Santa Barbara was 202.

Cibecue Apache (*see* Apache)

Citizen Potawatomi (*see* Potawatomi)

Clallam (*see* Klallam)

Clatskanie (*see* Klatskanie)

Clatsop (*see* Chinook)

Coast Miwok (*see* Miwok)

Cochiti Pueblo (*see* Pueblo)

Cocopa
Geographic Region:
Southwest (southeastern California)
Linguistic Group: Hokan-Yuman
Principal Dwelling Type: Domed bark, thatch or hide house
Principal Subsistence Type: Wild plants, small game, maize

Colville
Geographic Region: Great Basin (northeastern Washington and southern British Columbia)
Linguistic Group: Salishan
Principal Dwelling Type:
Semi-subterranean house
Principal Subsistence Type: Fish, game
Note: Subgroup of Spokane tribes

Comanche
Geographic Region: Plains and Prairies (northern Texas)

Linguistic Group: Uto-Aztecan
Principal Dwelling Type: Plains tipi
Principal Subsistence Type: Buffalo, other game

The Comanche are an offshoot of the Shoshone and one of several numanic speaking tribes. They are linguistically related to the Shoshone, Ute and Paiute, whose language is remotely related to Aztec. Their name comes from the Spanish *camino ancho,* which means 'wide trail.' They once lived in the Rocky Mountains near the Shoshone, but migrated to the plains to hunt buffalo. Though they became nomadic Plains Indians, they still maintained good relations with the Shoshone.

On the plains they ranged from the Platte River country of Nebraska south to the Texas panhandle. They formed alliances with the Caddo and Kiowa after the mid-eighteenth century, and about 1815 they began trading with the white settlers. In 1834 the Comanche, under Ishacoly (Traveling Wolf) and Tabequeva (Sun Eagle) met formally with the US Army, under Colonel Henry Dodge. The first treaty between the Comanche and the United States was signed on the Canadian River in August 1835.

The annexation of Texas and the California Gold Rush brought a great many white people through Comanche hunting grounds during the 1850s. This, along with a war with the Osage, resulted in a great deal of pressure on the Comanche, which in turn resulted in a number of hostile incidents. In 1859 portions of the Comanche tribe were settled under US government protection along the Washita River in present-day Oklahoma. During the Civil War, the Comanche signed treaties with both sides. However, by 1864 Comanche raids against travelers on the Santa Fe Trail brought about a US Army expedition against them led by Christopher 'Kit' Carson in which the Comanche were victorious. The hostilities continued until 1867, when the still undefeated Comanche signed the Medicine Lodge Creek Treaty, which gave them a sizable reservation in Indian Territory. By 1874 the drastic depletion of buffalo herds led to a final period of Comanche warfare that ended in June 1875.

By this time, Quanah Parker, the most well known of the Comanche chiefs, rose to prominence. Born in 1845, he was the son of Chief Nokoni of the Quahadi Comanche and Cynthia Ann Parker, a white woman who had been kidnapped as a child in Texas and who had grown up among the Comanche. Quanah Parker had a good reputation as both a warrior and leader among the Quahadi, a band of Comanche who had never been a signatory to any of the treaties. After the cessation of Comanche hostilities in 1875, Parker became the first recognized chief of all Comanche. He promoted adoption of elements of white civilization among his people and made numerous trips to Washington, DC as a Comanche delegate. He also served as one of three justices on the US Court of Indian Offenses, a tribunal acclaimed for both efficiency and fairness. He died in 1911 at Cache, Oklahoma where his home is now preserved as a historical site. His son, White Parker, went on to serve as a Methodist minister in Oklahoma.

In 1906, when Oklahoma became a state, the Comanche lands were the last to

Below Left: **Stone tools of the Chumash tribe, accomplished ocean fishermen who lived off the southern coastal waters of California.** *Below right:* **A Chitimacha basket woven by a method known as twilled plaiting. The coloration for these designs was derived from vegetable dyes, and applied to cane before it was skillfully woven.**

Left: **A George Catlin painting depicting a Comanche brave about to lance to death an enemy Osage. The Comanches were the rulers of the western plains and** were fanatical about war and horses. On horseback, they were unbeatable, in part owing to their ability to breed horses for speed and agility.

Opposite: **In 1891 these two Comanche girls from Oklahoma posed in their decorated buckskin dresses. The taller girl is the daughter of the great Comanche Chief Quanah Parker (*above*) whose mother, Cynthia Ann Parker, was a white captive. She was recaptured by the whites after 25 years.**

be opened to white settlement. Four years later Comanche numbers were estimated at 1476, down from 1553 in 1898. Population estimates in the nineteenth century show an increase from 1900 in 1851 to 2538 in 1869, but a decline to 1399 in 1880. In 1924 there were 1718, and in 1950 there were about 2700 Comanche on the Oklahoma reservation. In 1985 the

Comanche tribe on Oklahoma's Anadarko Agency numbered 3642.

Comox
Geographic Region: Northwest Coast (southwestern British Columbia mainland)
Linguistic Group: Salishan
Principal Dwelling Type: Rectangular plank house
Principal Subsistence Type: Fish
    In 1967 there were 783 Comox in Canada.

Conconcully (*see* Okinagan)

Conestoga (*see* Susquehannock)

Conoy (*see* Delaware)

Coos
Geographic Region: Northwest Coast (southern Oregon coast, adjacent to the site of present-day Coos Bay, Oregon)
Linguistic Group: Penutian (language isolate)
Principal Dwelling Type: Rectangular plank house
Principal Subsistence Type: Fish

Coosa (*see* Creek)

Copalis
Geographic Region: Northwest Coast (Washington coast)
Linguistic Group: Salishan
Principal Dwelling Type: Rectangular plank house
Principal Subsistence Type: Fish

Copper Eskimo (*see* Eskimo)

Costanoan (Ohlone)
Geographic Region: California (San Francisco Bay Area)
Linguistic Group: Uto-Aztecan
Principal Dwelling Type: Domed bark, thatch or hide house
Principal Subsistence Type: Acorns
    The Costanoans were the aboriginal people of the lands surrounding San Francisco Bay and extending south through the present-day Santa Clara Valley and into present Santa Cruz County. They were typical California hunters and gatherers for whom acorns provided the staple food source. The Costanoans interacted with the Pomo and Coast Miwok to the north and the Chumash to the south. Early estimates of their population are based on baptismal records of Mission San Francisco de Asis, which showed that 1087 Costonoans from the west side of the bay and 985 from the east were baptized between 1780 and 1821. This seems to indicate an average tribal population of about 3000 during that period.

Coeur d'Alene
Geographic Region: Great Basin (northern Idaho)
Linguistic Group: Salishan
Principal Dwelling Type:
    Semisubterranean house
Principal Subsistence Type: Large game

Note: Subgroup of Spokane tribes

Coweta (*see* Creek)

Cowichan
Geographic Region: Northwest Coast
Linguistic Group: Salishan
Principal Dwelling Type: Rectangular
  plank house
Principal Subsistence Type: Fish
   In 1967 there were 5652 Cowichan in
Canada.

Cowlitz
Geographic Region: Northwest Coast
  (southern Washington)
Linguistic Group: Salishan
Principal Dwelling Type:
  Semisubterranean house
Principal Subsistence Type: Fish
Subgroup: Upper Cowlitz (Penutian-
  Sahaptin speaking)

Cree
Geographic Region: Subarctic
  (Saskatchewan and Manitoba)
Linguistic Group: Algonquian
Principal Dwelling Type: Crude conical
  tipi
Principal Subsistence Type: Caribou,
  moose
   Geographically, the Cree were the
southernmost of the major subarctic
tribes, situated in an ideal trading location
between the Chipewyan to the north and
the Chippewa to the south. In addition to
trading with other tribes, the Cree developed early trading relations with the
French and English. Along with the Assiniboin, they were responsible for
pushing the Blackfoot out of western Saskatchewan. The Cree are still one of the
major tribes in Canada, with a 1967 population of 60,597.

Creek (Muskoke)
Geographic Region: Southeast (Georgia
  and Alabama)
Linguistic Group: Muskogean
Principal Dwelling Type: Rectangular
  thatched house

Creeks led by Shawnee Chief Tecumseh prepare to go
to war (*above*). He attempted to unite Eastern tribes
against the whites. The Creeks lost their battle for land
but, unlike some tribes, manage to retain their cultural
traditions even today (*right*).

Principal Subsistence Type: Maize

Subgroups: Abihki, Atasi, Coosa*, Coweta*, Eufaula, Hilabia, Kasihta* (Cusseta), Kolomi, Okchai, Pakana, Tukabahchee*

(*Foundation tribes of the Creek confederacy, the principal 'sticks' of the Creek Nation)

The Creek were originally one of the dominant tribes in the mid-south and later became known as one of the Five Civilized Tribes. They were known in their own language as Muskoke or Muskoge, by the Shawnee as Humaskogi, by the Delaware as Masquachki and by the British (c 1720) as the Ochese Creek Indians, hence the present name. Their name has been adapted for that of their linguistic group and for Muskogee, Oklahoma, which was a major city of the Creek Nation in Indian Territory.

The Creeks may have made contact with the Spanish as early as 1521, but they certainly were visited by De Soto in 1540. At this time, the Coosa were the dominant subgroup, but by 1700 the chief of the Coweta was referred to as the 'emperor of the Creek.' The Tukabahchee may have once been a separate tribe associated with the Shawnee. They were the most populous of the Creek subgroups, with an 1832 population of 1287.

From their dominant role in the mid-south, the Creeks were pushed westward from the Carolina/Georgia coast after their defeat by the British in the Yamassee War of 1715. By this time, however, other tribes such as the Alabama, Koasati, Natchez and Yuchi began to join the Creek confederacy.

During the American Revolution, the Creeks, under emperor Alexander McGillivray (son of a Scottish father and a Creek-French mother), were allied with the English, and McGillivray (1740–1793) served as a colonel in the British Army. After the war, however, McGillivray quickly befriended the victorious Americans.

White encroachment on Creek lands over the next quarter century led to bad feelings and official Creek neutrality in the War of 1812. Though officially neutral, some Creek bands, known as 'Red Sticks,' took the opportunity to begin raiding white settlements. This evolved into a full-scale civil war, known as the Red Stick War, with neutral Creeks as well as the whites. They sacked Tukabahchee Town and followed this with the massacre of Fort Mims in August 1813. The white men mobilized and met the red sticks on the Tallapoosa River in the decisive battle of the war. On 27 March 1814,

the US Army, under General Andrew Jackson and the then pro-American Creeks under Coweta head chief William McIntosh, defeated the Red Sticks in the Battle of Horseshoe Bend.

The Red Sticks were beaten, but the serious divisions in the Creek Nation continued, as did the violence, and Chief McIntosh himself was shot and killed in May 1825. The internal warfare spilled over into white settlements, and this added fuel to American public sentiment for a removal of all Indians to west of the Mississippi. Some Creeks, such as those under Chief Opotheyahola, agreed to the move to Indian Territory as early as 1832, but it was not until 1840 that the two major Creek factions were reunited in the government of the Creek Nation.

During the American Civil War, the Creeks were once again divided. Opothleyahola's band attempted to leave the Confederate-dominated Indian Territory for Union-held Kansas, but they were overtaken by Confederate troops and badly mauled. When the Indian governments of Indian Territory were reconstituted in 1866, the entire western portion of the Creek Nation was ceded back to the US government for use by other tribes. The Creek Nation, along with the other nations of the territory, was dissolved in 1906 when the state of Oklahoma came into existence.

The Creek population at the time of their removal to Indian Territory in 1832 was 21,733, and by 1847 it had grown to 14,888. In 1915 there were 11,967 Creek still in Oklahoma, and in 1944 there were 9900. In 1985 the Creek tribe at the Okmulgee Agency in Oklahoma numbered 42,519.

Croatan

Geographic Region: Northeast (Roanoke Island, Virginia)
Linguistic Group: Algonquian
Principal Dwelling Type: Rectangular barrel-roofed house
Principal Subsistence Type: Maize

The name Croatan has been found carved on a tree at the site of the Sir Walter Raleigh colony, perhaps a clue to the disappearance of the colonists in 1591.

Crow (Absaroka)

Geographic Region: Plains and Prairies (Knife River, North Dakota)
Linguistic Group: Siouan
Principal Dwelling Type: Plains tipi
Principal Subsistence Type: Buffalo and other game

The Crow legends indicate that the tribe once was associated with the Hidatsa

Delegates from 34 tribes in front of the Creek Council House in 1880 Indian Territory (*top*); World War II Congressional Medal of Honor awardee Lt Ernest Childers (*far left*), a Creek who wiped out two machinegun nests in Italy, is congratulated by Gen Jacob Devers; Creek tribesmen make a goal during a traditional game of ball in 1938 (*left*); a Crow burial platform (*above*). This kept animals away from the body.

Curley (*above*) was a Crow scout for the Seventh Cavalry detachment led by Colonel George Armstrong Custer at the Battle of the Little Bighorn. He was one of the few survivors of the June 1876 battle in which Custer and over 200 of his troops were killed by an overwhelming force of Sioux and Cheyenne. Crow Chief Plenty Coups (*opposite*) led his forces to fight beside the US Army against the Sioux. The Crow often worked with the US Army against their traditional rivals, the Sioux.

in the Knife River country, but migrated west to the Yellowstone River drainage in Montana during the late seventeenth or early eighteenth century. Their name, Absaroka, translates as 'children of the large-beaked bird,' so early white traders in the region referred to them as the Crow people.

Below: **Crow prisoners under guard by the US Army at Crow Agency, Montana in 1887.**

Like other Plains Indians, the Crow depended on the buffalo for their food, clothing and shelter. They traded sporadically with the white man throughout the first part of the nineteenth century, but as the buffalo population began to decline, the Crow became more dependent on whites. By the terms of the Fort Laramie Treaty in May 1868, they were consolidated onto a reservation in southeastern Montana in the central part of the lands

they were inhabiting.

An important part of the religious and social life of the Crow was the annual Sun Dance, which was banned along with all other Indian religious ceremonies by the US government in 1904. It was revived in modified form after 1941.

Development of oil lands contained within the Crow reservation in the 1970s brought a badly needed income into tribal coffers. In 1970 there were 3500 people

living on the Crow Reservation in Montana, and by 1985 there were 5811.

Cumumbah (*see* Ute)

Cupeño
Geographic Region: Southwest (southeastern California)
Linguistic Group: Uto-Aztecan
Principal Dwelling Type: Domed bark, thatch or hide house

Principal Subsistence Type: Wild plants, maize, small game

Known as one of the 'mission peoples' tribes, the Cupeño, who numbered roughly 500 at the time of the arrival of the Spanish, adapted early on to life at the Spanish mission settlements.

Dakota (*see* Sioux)

Delaware (Lenni-Lenape)
Geographic Region: Northeast (New Jersey, Pennsylvania, Delaware, Virginia)
Linguistic Group: Algonquian
Principal Dwelling Type: Rectangular barrel-roofed house
Principal Subsistence Type: Maize
Subgroups: Conoy, Munsee, Nanticoke (Moor), Unalachtigo, Unami

Delaware is an English name adapted from the river named for Lord de la Warr. It was applied to the Indians who called themselves Lenni-Lenape, meaning 'men of of our nation,' and who were called Loupe ('wolves') by the early French because of their fierce fighting ability. In 1682 they sold land to, and concluded an important peace treaty with, William Penn in Pennsylvania. In the early eighteenth century, they participated briefly in the Iroquois League. Though their original lands were along the Atlantic coast, by 1750 some of the Delaware had settled among the Huron in Ohio.

In 1778, the Delaware signed the first treaty concluded between the United States and an Indian tribe, granting them representation in Congress. By 1794, however, the Delaware and the United States were at war, and on 20 August the Delaware were defeated by General 'Mad Anthony' Wayne in the Battle of Fallen Timbers in Ohio. A peace treaty was signed on 3 August 1795 at Greenville, Ohio granting the Delaware the right to live in Ohio. All of this was ceded back to the United States by 1829 and the Delaware moved first to eastern Kansas, and then south to Indian Territory. In 1839 the Delaware national government was established with the Delaware population living in the Choctaw Nation and (until 1866) in Kansas. After 1867 the 985 regis-

tered Delaware living in Kansas moved south to the Caney River area where they became citizens of the Cherokee Nation, was sent their children to Cherokee schools. Though they were to suffer some discrimination among the Cherokee, the Delaware occasionally were elected to serve on the Cherokee Nation Council.

The Delaware tribal population is said to have been about 2400 in 1823, and 2200 in 1906, and increased to roughly 3000 in the mid-nineteenth century. In 1950 there were 2162 Delaware in Oklahoma including about 1250 descendants of the registered Delaware from Kansas. In 1985 there were 396 members of the Delaware tribe at the Anadarko Agency in Oklahoma.

Diegueño
Geographic Region:
  Southwestern California (San Diego)
Linguistic Group: Hokan-Yuman
Principal Dwelling Type: Domed bark, thatch or hide house
Principal Subsistence Type: Acorns

The Diegueños were among the more populous of Southern California Indian tribes prior to the arrival of the Spanish, numbering about 3000 according to Alfred Kroeber's 1925 estimate. By 1882, however, the effects of disease and intermarriage had reduced their number to 731.

Digger (*see* Maidu)

Dineh (*see* Navajo)

Dogrib (Thlingchadinne)
Geographic Region: Subarctic (Great Bear Lake, MacKenzie Territory)
Linguistic Group: Athapascan
Principal Dwelling Type: Crude conical tipi
Principal Subsistence Type: Caribou, moose

Duwamish
Geographic Region: Northwest Coast (Puget Sound, Washington)
Linguistic Group: Salishan
Principal Dwelling Type: Rectangular plank house
Principal Subsistence Type: Fish

The Duwamish were noted for their ceremonial spirit canoe ceremony, which was staged by shamans during the winter to recapture souls that might become lost enroute to the spirit world. The ceremony involved songs and ceremonial dance as well as the shaman's magic, and was paid for by the relatives of the person whose soul was lost.

Eastern Shawnee (*see* Shawnee)

East Greenland Eskimo (*see* Eskimo)

Eel River
Geographic Region: Northeast (Indiana, Ohio)
Linguistic Group: Algonquian
Principal Dwelling Type: Domed bark, thatch or hide house
Principal Subsistence Type: Maize

A small tribe associated with the Eel River region, they sold their reservation in Boone County, Indiana in 1828 and merged with the Miami. Some of their descendants may still be found among the Miami in Oklahoma. (*See also* Miami)

Erie
Geographic Region: Northeast (Lake Erie region)
Linguistic Group: Iroquoian
Principal Dwelling Type:
Rectangular barrel-roofed house
Principal Subsistence Type: Maize

Though related to the Iroquois, the Erie were never members of the Iroquois League, and their dialect was similar to that of the Huron. Their name means 'at the place of the panther,' and possibly for this reason they were called 'cat' Indians by early whites. The tribe was almost completely wiped out by the Iroquois Confederacy in 1656. The survivors joined the Conestoga and Seneca, and through the mid-twentieth century a handful of them still survived among the Seneca in Oklahoma.

Eskimo (Inuit)
Geographic Region: Arctic
Linguistic Group:
Eskimo-Aleut (Eskaleutian)
Principal Dwelling Type:
Rectangular earth-covered Alaskan house: MacKenzie, North Alaskan, St Lawrence Island, South Alaskan and West Alaskan Eskimos
Igloo: Baffin Island, Caribou, Copper, Iglulik, Labrador, Netsilik, Polar and Southampton Eskimos
Domed stone-earth-whalebone house: East Greenland, Labrador and West Greenland Eskimos

Principal Subsistence Type:
Fish, sea mammals, caribou, moose: MacKenzie, South Alaskan and West Alaskan Eskimos
Sea Mammals, caribou and moose: Caribou, Copper, Iglulik, Labrador, Netsilik, North Alaskan and Southampton Eskimos
Sea mammals: Baffin Island, East Greenland, Polar, St Lawrence Island and Polar Eskimos
Subgroups: Baffin Island (Sallumiut, Takamiut), Caribou, Copper, Iglulik, Labrador, MacKenzie, Netsilik, North Alaskan (Kanianigmiut, Kobukmiut, Kugmiut, Natakmiut, Nunamiut, Point Hope, Selawikmiut and Utukokmiut), Polar, St Lawrence Island, South Alaskan, Southampton, West Alaskan (Kaviagmiut, Kinugmiut, Malemiut, Unaligmiut) and West Greenland Eskimos

The Eskimos call themselves Inuit, or 'the people.' The name Eskimo, meaning 'eaters of a raw flesh,' was given to them by the Algonquian-speaking peoples to the south. The Eskimo land and culture stretch for 6000 miles across the shores of the Arctic Ocean, from Siberia to Greenland, encompassing some of the most rugged territory in the world. In other areas of similar size within the continent, it would not be uncommon to encounter a

Resourceful Eskimo women: A mother with her child on her back keeps out Alaska's chill with furs (*top right*). The fur is turned inward to provide insulation. An industrious grandmother (*middle right*) sews skins into garments; besides preparing a seafood dinner for her family, this woman (*below*) must first catch the fish through a hole she has cut in the ice. Only men are allowed to hunt bigger game.

Eskimo artifacts: Simple tools used with great care shaped familiar animal likenesses such as this seal sculpted from bone (*left*); a crow mask (*above, top*) carved from scarce driftwood by an Eskimo man under the direction of a shaman during the long winter nights; two soapstone human figures (*above*) — these originally sat on an ivory sled pulled by ivory dogs. Eskimos were well known for the tiny figurines, toys and charms they created and also for their skill in decorating everyday functional tools, weapons and utensils.

Facing page: **Using a hand-fashioned drill 'powered' by a bow and leather thong device, an Alaskan Eskimo carves figures from chunks of ivory.** *Above:* **An Eskimo dance band using drumheads made from whale stomachs.** *Left:* **Eskimos building an igloo in Arctic Canada around 1918.** *Below left:* **Aleutian Eskimos in an umiak dressing a whale.**

long winters, both story telling and shamanic religion were well developed among the Eskimo. The Eskimo also have well-developed visual arts; walrus and whale bone ivory are a favored media for both decorative and religious art, as well as for such practical implements as harpoons.

The Eskimo inhabit a region of the continent where the white man is still a newcomer, but his influence has certainly been felt in the latter part of the twentieth century, as Eskimo now go on hunting trips in motorized umiaks and carrying rifles. The development of oil land on Alaska's North Slope during the 1960s and 1970s brought an influx of white people to a traditional Eskimo area.

The total Eskimo population of Alaska and Canada was estimated at 43,846 in 1970. In 1985 in Alaska, there were 9550 people at the Nome Indian Agency; 11,283 at the Fairbanks Agency; 12,883 at the Bethel Agency; 11,177 in the Cook Inlet Native Association; 693 in the Copper River Native Association; and 1443 in the North Pacific Rim Association.

Euchee (*see* Yuchi)

Eufaula (*see* Creek)

Eyak
Geographic Region: Northwest Coast (southernmost central Alaska)
Linguistic Group: Eyak (a Na-Dene language related to Haidan and Athapascan)
Principal Dwelling Type: Double lean-to
Principal Subsistence Type: Fish

multitude of languages and cultures, but throughout the entire Arctic the Eskimo language is virtually the same.

The Eskimo probably arrived in North America from Asia via the Bering land bridge in 3000 BC or before, and their culture has remained largely the same ever since.

The Eskimo livelihood revolves around the sea mammals of the Arctic Ocean such as whales, walruses and seals, which are hunted for food, clothing and fuel. Eskimos live in a variety of types of houses,

with the domed ice house, or igloo, being characteristic. Traditional transportation for the Eskimo included dogsleds for traveling over ice or snow and hide-covered boats for traveling at sea. The latter range from the small one-man kayak to the large umiak, which is used for whaling expeditions.

During the long, dark arctic winter, Eskimo life turns inward toward small villages where entire families live in one-room houses amid piles of polar bear and muskox hides. Not surprising, given the

Fernandeño

Geographic Region:
Southeastern California
Linguistic Group: Uto-Aztecan
Principal Dwelling Type:
Domed bark, thatch or hide house
Principal Subsistence Type: Acorns

Known as one of the 'mission peoples' tribes, the Fernandeño, along with the Gabrieleño and San Nicoleño, had a population of about 5000 prior to the arrival of the Spanish.

Five Civilized Tribes (*see* Cherokee, Chickasaw, Choctaw, Creek and Seminole)

Flathead

Geographic Region: Great Basin (western Montana)
Linguistic Group: Salishan
Principal Dwelling Type: Bark-covered huts, plains tipi

Principal Subsistence Type: Buffalo and other large game

The Flathead, a subgroup of the Spokane tribes, were given their name from a custom common to many Salishan people of practicing head deformation by strapping their infants to hard cradleboards. This flattened the back of the head and made the top appear more round. The Flathead, conversely, did not practice head flattening, and therefore the tops of their heads were flatter than those of other Salishan peoples, hence the name.

Because of their proximity to the plains, the Flathead developed some of the cultural traits of the tribes residing there. For example, they were known for their horsemanship and, when on a hunt, they used plains-type buffalo-hide tipi.

The traditional range of the Flathead was in the area surrounding present-day Flathead Lake in western Montana, and their present reservation is immediately to the south of the lake. The 1985 population of that reservation was 3225, up from 2900 in 1970.

Facing page: **A delegation of Flathead Indians congregated with their interpreter in Washington in 1884. Their traditional range was in western Montana where they practiced skilled horsemanship. They were eventually forced into Canada when whites settled in Montana.** *Below:* **Flathead Indians in a parade on Higgins Avenue in Missoula, Montana in 1955.**

Forest Potawatomi (*see* Potawatomi)

Fox (Mesquaki, Muskwaki)

Geographic Region: Northeast (Illinois)
Linguistic Group: Algonquian
Principal Dwelling Type: Domed bark, thatch or hide house
Principal Subsistence Type: Hunting, maize

Originally called Mesquaki, or 'red earth people,' the Fox took their present name from the French who observed that they had a fox clan within the tribal structure. Unlike many other tribes around the Great Lakes, the Fox were not on friendly terms with the French, and were constantly at war with them. A major defeat at the hands of the French in 1716 only seemed to intensify the hostilities, but another defeat in 1730 practically wiped out the tribe. The remainder joined their kinsmen, the Sauk, who lived in the Green Bay area, and continued the hostilities until 1740 when the Sauk and Fox made peace with the French.

By the early nineteenth century, the Fox were living along the Rock River in northern Illinois. In 1940 there were still 400 Fox near Tama, Iowa and about 475 near Stroud, Oklahoma. In 1985 the combined population of Sauk and Fox was 745 in Iowa, 56 on their joint reservation in Kansas, and 1041 in Oklahoma.

Gabrieleño
Geographic Region:
    Southeastern California
Linguistic Group: Uto-Aztecan
Principal Dwelling Type: Domed bark,
    thatch or hide house
Principal Subsistence Type:
    Acorns, maize
    Known as one of the 'mission peoples'
tribes, the Gabrieleño, along with the San
Nicoleño, had a combined population of
about 5000 prior to the arrival of the
Spanish.

Gosiute
Geographic Region: Great Basin (north-
    ern Nevada and Utah)
Linguistic Group: Uto-Aztecan
Principal Dwelling Type: Crude conical
    tipi
Principal Subsistence Type: Wild plants,
    small game
    The Gosiute were one of several nu-
manic speaking tribes, who intermixed
with, and were related to, the Bannock,
Paiute, Shoshone and Ute tribes.

Great Osage (*see* Osage)

Green River Snake (*see* Shoshone)

Gros Ventre (Atsina)
Geographic Region:
    Plains and Prairies (North Dakota and
        southern Saskatchewan)
Linguistic Group: Siouan
Principal Dwelling Type: Plains tipi
Principal Subsistence Type: Buffalo
Subgroups: Hidatsa, Awatixa, Awaxawi
    and Atsina Proper

Guale
Geographic Region: Southeast (Georgia)
Linguistic Group: Muskogean
Principal Dwelling Type:
    Rectangular thatched house
Principal Subsistence Type: Maize

Left: **Angelic La Moose, whose grandfather was a
Flathead chief, wearing a costume made by her
mother. A canvas-covered Plains-style conical tipi is in
the background of this 1913 photograph. Angelic is
standing on a beautifully woven rug reminiscent of
Navajo weavings. Art was important even though subsistence work took up much of their time.**

Haida totem poles at Old Kassan Village in southeastern Alaska. Poles in foreground show the crests of Chief Skowl who died in 1882. The literal translation of this crest is: 'raven stealing the sun; raven putting back his beak after having lost it on the hook of the halibut fisherman; grizzly bear and the young woman or the cubs.'

Haida (Hyda, Kaigani)

Geographic Region: Northwest Coast (Queen Charlotte Islands)

Linguistic Group: Haidan (A Na-Dene language related to Athapascan)

Principal Dwelling Type: Rectangular plank house

Principal Subsistence Type: Fish

The Haida were the aboriginal people of the Queen Charlotte Islands, major islands offshore from British Columbia and immediately south of the Alaska panhandle. They had a highly developed culture, and lived in villages of large, cedar plank houses dominated by 50-foot totem poles. They fished and hunted sea mammals from huge cedar log canoes. The Haida were particularly noted in the region for their intricately carved totem poles and canoes. Like most people of the Northwest Coast, their staple was salmon, but other fish such as halibut were also taken.

The Haida were prolific traders and had a highly developed concept of wealth and nobility. For this reason, the practice of the potlatch was especially important to the Haida. The potlatch was a ceremony practiced by many of the Northwest Coast tribes, an enormous celebration in which a nobleman would entertain guests and give them gifts. The success of the potlatch was determined by how long it lasted and how many gifts were given, as much as by how good a time the guests had. As a result, a noble might accumulate wealth for years and his potlatch might last for days. A person's place in Haida society would be greatly enhanced by a successful potlatch. With the arrival of the white man and his mass-produced goods, the potlatches got out of hand, and a delicate balance was disturbed threatening not only the relations between

the Indians and the white man but the fabric of Northwest Coast Indian society itself. From 1884 until 1951, when all mention of it was stricken from books, the potlatch was illegal in Canada.

The first Haida contact with white men came in 1774 when the Spanish explored the Queen Charlotte Islands. Later, the Haida were visited by Americans and by the English, including Captain Cook. Smallpox became a serious problem in the late eighteenth and early twentieth centuries, and the Haida population of over 6000 in 1835 fell to barely 800 in 1885. By 1915 the population had been reduced to 588, but thereafter it began to increase. In 1968 the population of Masset and Skidegate, the major Haida population centers on the Queen Charlotte Islands, was over 1500.

Opposite: **A portrait of Black Moccasin of the Hidatsa tribe as painted by George Catlin in 1823. Catlin spent six years among the Western tribes. His paintings of Plains tribemembers have since become major reference sources of anthropological interest.** *Below:* **Smaller artifacts of the Northwest coastal tribes are as notable for their rich symbolism and intricate craftship as their more widely known totem poles. This carved musical instrument was produced by the Haida.**

Hainai

Geographic Region: Plains and Prairies (Texas)
Linguistic Group: Caddoan
Principal Dwelling Type: Thatched house
Principal Subsistence Type: Maize

The Hainai were related to the Caddo and affiliated with the Hasininai confederacy of Caddoan-speaking people of southeastern Texas. Their name comes from *nayano,* which is Caddoan for 'people.' The Hainai were noted by De Soto in 1542 and La Salle in 1687 as living in the Brazos River country in Texas. Their village in present-day Nacogdoches County was an important site of intertribal religious ceremonies, and was later the site of a Catholic mission established in 1716. During the Civil War, the Hainai sided with the Confederacy. After the war they joined the Wichita-Caddo Reservation. The tribe was last counted as a separate tribe in 1876, at which time it had a population of 30, down from 150 counted in 1864.

Haisla

Geographic Region: Northwest Coast (British Columbia)
Linguistic Group: Wakashan (related to Salishan)
Principal Dwelling Type: Rectangular plank house
Principal Subsistence Type: Fish

Though presently living at the heads of the Douglas and Gardner channels, Haisla legend has this tribe originating in Rivers Inlet. They are related to the Kwakiutl, Heiltsuk and Bella Bella. A Haisla girl is credited with the invention of the *yakatl,* a type of net used for coastal fishing. It was tubular, with a funnel-shaped mouth that could be closed with a ring and pole. The *yakatl* was introduced to the Tsimshian and later to the Tlingit and other tribes. In 1967 there were 768 Haisla living in Canada.

Halchidhoma

Geographic Region: Southwest
Linguistic Group: Uto-Aztecan
Principal Dwelling Type: Domed bark, thatch or hide house
Principal Subsistence Type: Wild plants, small game

The Halchidhoma lived near the Mojave in the lower Colorado River country along the present California-Arizona

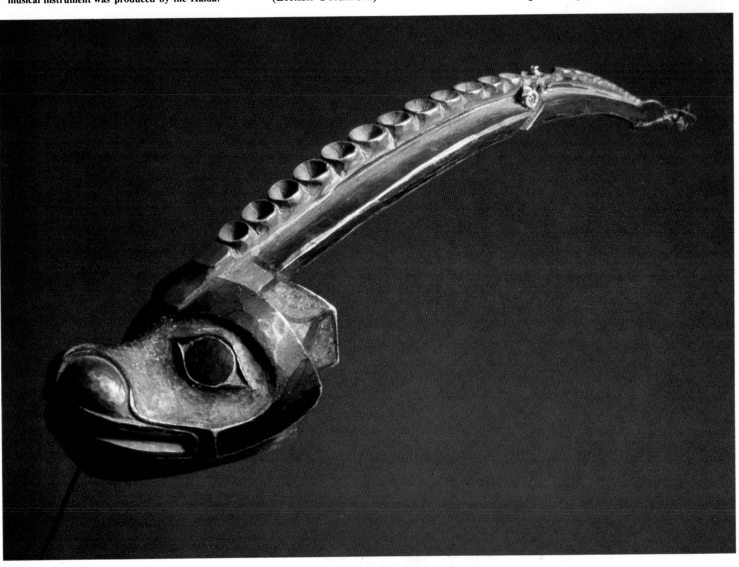

border. Alfred Kroeber estimates that at their peak, the two tribes had a total population of 3500, of which 950 lived in present-day California.

Han

Geographic Region: Subarctic (north Alaska interior)
Linguistic Group: Athapascan
Principal Dwelling Type:
    Rectangular earth-covered Alaskan house, double lean-to
Principal Subsistence Type:
    Fish, caribou, moose

Hare

Geographic Region: Subarctic (Great Bear Lake, MacKenzie Territory)
Linguistic Group: Athapascan
Principal Dwelling Type: Double lean-to; crude conical tipi
Principal Subsistence Type:
    Caribou, moose

Known in their own language as Kaw-chodinneh, the Hare were typical Subarctic hunters who followed the caribou herds in the Canadian north. In 1967 their population was 679.

Havasupai (Supai)

Geographic Region: Southwest (Arizona)
Linguistic Group: Hokan
Principal Dwelling Type: Crude conical tipi
Principal Subsistence Type: Wild plants, maize

The Havasupai people were among the aboriginal people of the Grand Canyon region. They are known for their pottery

and a superior grade of red ocher that they mined in the Grand Canyon up through the seventeenth century. They traded the ocher with the Hopi as far east as the Santa Fe Pueblo. The Havasupai are presently associated with the Truxton Canyon Agency in Arizona, where in 1985 they numbered 430.

Heiltsuk

Geographic Region: Northwest Coast (mainland coast of British Columbia)
Linguistic Group: Wakashan
Principal Dwelling Type:
    Rectangular plank house
Principal Subsistence Type: Fish

The Heiltsuk were part of a related linguistic group that included the Bella Bella and a number of small bands called the Xaihai. This group in turn was related linguistically to the Kwakiutl, and they traded with the Bella Coola as well as the Kwakiutl. In 1967 there were still 1198

Below: **A Hopi woman in the early 1900s styles the elaborate 'squash blossom' coiffure that advertised a young girl's availability for marriage. The style was bestowed as proof of household skill. The complex bun hairstyle wrapped around a U-shaped bow could take over an hour to arrange. After she marries, this girl will braid her hair simply.**

Heiltsuk fishing the Northwest Pacific coast.

Henya (*see* Tlingit)

Hidatsa (*see* Gros Ventre)

Hilabia (*see* Creek)

Hill Patwin (*see* Patwin)

Hill Wintun (*see* Wintun)

Hitchiti

Geographic Region: Southeast (Georgia)
Linguistic Group: Muskogean
Principal Dwelling Type:
   Rectangular thatched house
Principal Subsistence Type: Maize

The name Hitchiti comes from the Creek *ahit'chita* meaning to 'look up the stream.' Although their languages differed, the Hitchiti were associated with the Creek tribe and they were removed to Indian Territory at the same time. In 1832 there were nine Hitchiti towns in the Georgia/North Florida area with a population of 2036. After their removal to Indian Territory, they lived among the Creek and were gradually absorbed by the Creek Nation. Three Hitchiti-speaking men—Legus Perryman, Samuel Checote and Pleasant Porter—served as principal chief of the Creek Nation during the nineteenth century. Though the tribe eventually merged with the Creek, the 1891 Creek census listed 182 Hitchiti still living at the town of the same name in the Creek Nation.

Hoh

Geographic Region: Northwest Coast
   (Washington coast)
Linguistic Group: Salishan
Principal Dwelling Type:
   Rectangular plank house
Principal Subsistence Type: Fish

Hohokam (prehistoric ancestors of the Pima and Papago tribes) (*see* Puma, Papago)

Honeches (*see* Waco)

Hoonah (*see* Tlingit)

Hoopa (*see* Hupa)

Hootznahoo (*see* Tlingit)

Hopi

Geographic Region: Southwest (Arizona,
   Colorado, New Mexico)
Linguistic Group: Uto-Aztecan

Principal Dwelling Type:
   Rectangular adobe house (pueblo)
Principal Subsistence Type: Maize, wild plants

The Hopi, whose name comes from *hopitu* meaning 'the peaceful ones,' are traditionally associated culturally with the Zuñi and with the Pueblo Indians *(see also* Pueblo). All of these people live in pueblos or cities comprised of a complex of sometimes multistoried, rectangular houses. The name pueblo derives from the Spanish word for 'people.'

The Hopi are descendants of people who migrated into the Southwest prior to 1000 BC. By 700 AD they had developed agriculture and were raising corn, beans, squash and cotton. By 1100 AD they had abandoned their aboriginal pit houses for multi-level adobe houses, and had founded cities at Oraibi and Mesa Verde. Coronado reached the area in 1541, and his arrival was followed by an influx of Spanish explorers and missionaries. In 1680 the Pueblo Indians revolted against the Spanish and in the wake of this revolt, the Hopi population moved to the tops of mesas such as Antelope and Black mesas, where smaller Hopi settlements already existed. The Hopi towns were autonomous, self-governing units headed by a chief.

The focus of Hopi cultural and religious activity was the Kachina ceremony. The Kachinas were spirits associated with the annual cycle of birth, death and rebirth. They lived underground from October through April and moved among

Above: **A Hupa tribesman from Northwest California measures an armslength of dentalia shells which, in 1900 when this photograph was taken, were often used as money. The shell necklaces were usually worn as a sign of wealth. Showing off one's riches was acceptable and, in many cases, expected.**

the people the rest of the year. During the Kachina ceremony, which was a coming-of-age ritual for all Hopi children, Hopi men dressed in elaborate masks and costumes to impersonate a specific Kachina. Dolls were also used to represent Kachinas, and today Kachina dolls (both antique and contemporary) are among the most valued of American Indian artifacts. All of the Hopi men belonged to a Kachina cult and some cities had as many as six cults, each with its own *kiva,* or church.

In the mid-nineteenth century, it was the Navajo rather than the white man that first threatened Hopi autonomy, and warfare between the two tribes continued through most of the century. A Hopi reservation was set aside in 1882, but the members of the tribe were split over whether to join. It was not until 1906 that all factions of the tribe accepted the reservation. Because the Hopi and Navajo reservations were established on overlapping lands, the conflict between the two tribes continued well into the twentieth century, with the boundaries of the respective reservations being redrawn several times up until as late as the 1970s.

The population of the Hopi Reservation grew from roughly 5000 in 1900 to 8952 in 1985.

The Katchina dolls (*opposite and above*) represent two Hopi spirits. The dolls are carved from cottonwood, painted and decorated with feathers or shells. After elaborate ceremonites the dolls are presented to children of the tribe for study. There is a different doll for each spirit.

Houeches (*see* Waco)

Housetonic (Stockbridge)
Geographic Region:
  Northeast (Massachusetts)
Linguistic Group: Algonquian
Principal Dwelling Type:
  Rectangular barrel-roofed house
Principal Subsistence Type:
  Hunting, maize
  The Housetonic was a small tribe that associated itself with the Oneida in the eighteenth century. In 1832 they joined in a confederation with the Munsee to purchase a tract of land in Wisconsin, where many still live. Others moved to Indian

Territory in 1867 and settled among the Cherokee. In 1985 the Stockbridge-Munsee community in Wisconsin had a population of 799.

Huanchane (*see* Waco)

Humptulips
Geographic Region: Northwest Coast
  (Southwestern Washington)
Linguistic Group: Salishan
Principal Dwelling Type:
  Rectangular plank house
Principal Subsistence Type: Fish

Hunkpapa (*see* Sioux)

Hupa (Hoopa)
Geographic Region:
  Northwest California
Linguistic Group: Athapascan
Principal Dwelling Type:
  Rectangular plank house
Principal Subsistence Type: Mix of animal and wild plant foods
  Like most California tribes, the acorn was a staple of the Hupa diet, but the tribe also hunted deer, which were abundant in the forests, and fished the salmon from the Northern California rivers. The position of chief was more important in Hupa tribal structure than with additional California tribes, but other levels of

Opposite: **In the 1890s two Hupa chiefs carrying sacred obsidian knives begin the White Deerskin Dance which was part of the World Renewal ceremony.** *Above:* **A Mohawk woman weaves a basket before a birch canoe.** *Above right:* **Mohawk chief Thayendanega, also known as Joseph Brandt.**

hierarchy were important primarily during ceremonies.

The Hupa village was semipermanent and contained two types of houses. The first was about 20 feet square with the center excavated to about five feet, and was used for sleeping and storage. The second type was a smaller sweat lodge, similar to the European sauna, and was used by the men.

The Hupa were concentrated in the Hoopa Valley of the lower Trinity River country and had a relatively higher population density than any of the neighboring California tribes. This density was 5.2 persons per square mile, compared to 2.4 for the Karok and 4.7 for the Yurok. Population data for the Hoopa Valley Reservation shows a dramatic increase from 623 in 1867 to 975 in 1869, probably owing to scattered individuals moving onto the reservation. From 1869 to 1877 the population declined to 427, and remained below 510 until after the turn of the century. There were 1345 people counted in 1914, and 1927 in 1928. In 1970 there were 1271 Hupas on the reservation, and in 1985 there were 2020.

Huron (*see* Wyandot)

Hyda (*see* Haida)

Iglulik Eskimo (*see* Eskimo)

Illinois
Geographic Region: Northeast (Illinois)
Linguistic Group: Algonquian
Principal Dwelling Type: Domed bark, thatch or hide house
Principal Subsistence Type: Hunting, maize
Subgroups: Cahokia, Kaskaskia, Michigamea, Moingwena, Peoria (Peouaria) and Tamaroa

The Illinois, whose name derives from *Illiniwek* meaning 'men,' were a confederation of Algonquian peoples related to the Miami. They were first encountered by white men in 1673 during the explorations of Father Jacques Marquette in what is today Illinois River country. The winter quarters of the entire tribe and subgroups were at Lake Peoria, as noted by La Salle in 1680. Shortly after La Salle's visit, the Illinois were attacked and badly beaten by the Iroquois, who had obtained firearms from the Dutch. The Illinois remained in their original homelands under the protection of the French until 1699 when (except

for the Peoria) they moved to the confluence of the Mississippi and Kaskasia rivers. Prior to 1680 the Illinois had numbered as many as 9000, but by the early nineteenth century only about 150 remained. This group settled in Kansas in 1832, and their descendants resettled in Indian Territory in 1867.

In 1818, meanwhile, 11 remaining Peoria signed a treaty with the United States. They allied with remaining Kaskaskia and caught up with the other Illinois in 1832. After arriving in these new lands, they formed closer cultural relations with the Piankashaw than with the other Illinois. In 1873, after having been moved to Indian Territory in 1867, the Peoria joined the Miami in a new confederation. In 1945 the United Peoria and Miami of the Quapaw Agency in Oklahoma numbered 413, of which 150 lived on the reservation. In 1985 the Peoria (excluding the Miami) numbered 398 at the reservation.

Inde (*see* Apache)

Ingalik
Geographic Region: Subarctic (Yukon and Kuskokwin rivers, central Alaska)
Linguistic Group: Athapascan
Principal Dwelling Type: Rectangular earth-covered Alaskan house
Principal Subsistence Type:
Caribou, moose, fish

The Ingalik were noted for making wooden bowls and oval-shaped, coiled baskets.

Above: **A modern Seneca mask made almost entirely of braided and sewn corn husks. Members of the Husk Face Society, a small religious group, wore these masks and danced during the Midwinter ceremonies that prophesied plentiful crops. Many** ceremonies were thought to be necessary to ensure a good harvest. Corn, of course, was one of the most important crops to the Seneca who depended upon it for sustenance.

Inuit (*see* Eskimo)

Iowa

Geographic Region: Plains and Prairies
Linguistic Group: Siouan-Chiewere
Principal Dwelling Type:
    Prairie-Southwest earth lodge
Principal Subsistence Type:
    Hunting, maize

The Iowa name is derived from the tribal term *Ai'yuwe,* which means 'marrow,' not 'the sleepy ones' as once

was thought. The Iowa were first encountered by the French in 1701 near the mouth of the Blue Earth River in Minnesota, but their range extended south as far as present-day Des Moines. They were related to the Winnebago and traded with many tribes of the region. They were especially noted for pipes carved of red pipestone that they took from a quarry in Minnesota.

In 1836 the Iowa were assigned a reservation in Kansas. By 1880 some of the

Above: See-non-ty-a, an Iowa medicine man, who posed for George Catlin in 1829. The medicine man was not a chief but was held in high esteem by his tribe and often led the search for new land. By this time his tribe has been pushed out of the area that is now named for them.

Iowa were living on Sauk and Fox lands in Indian Territory, and in 1883 they were granted their own reservation there. In 1760 there were an estimated 1100 Iowas, but by 1843 there were only 470, and in 1901 there were 88 listed as living among the Sauk and Fox. In 1985 there were 155 Iowa living at the Shawnee Agency in Oklahoma and 328 living on the Iowa Reservation in Kansas and Nebraska.

Iroquois

Geographic Region: Eastern and Central (New York State)

Linguistic Group: Iroquoian

Principal Dwelling Type:
   Rectangular barrel-roofed house

Principal Subsistence Type: Beans, maize, squash and wild animals

Subgroups: Cayuga, Mohawk, Oneida, Onandaga, Seneca

The Iroquois League, or Five Nations of the Iroquois, was the most powerful Indian military alliance in the eastern part of North America and probably the most successful alliance of any kind between so many important tribes. There were three principal clans—deer, turtle and wolf —existing within the five nations, and this was probably an important unifying factor in the league. The league was formed in the late sixteenth century at which time the five nations had a combined population of 7000.

The idea for the alliance was prompted by the bloodshed suffered by the five nations in intertribal conflicts. The fathers of the league were Chiefs Degamawida and Hiawatha, who were aided by Chiefs Jikonasa and Totadaho. The league was called the 'Great Peace' or the 'Long House,' the latter based on the long, rectangular houses in which the Iroquois people lived. The league was governed by a Great Council, in which the Mohawk and Seneca formed the upper house and the Oneida and Cayuga the lower house. The Onandaga provided the presiding officer and intervened when there was a tie vote. The individual nations could, and frequently did, make war as separate powers. In 1710 the Tuscaroras were admitted as a sixth nation without voting rights in the Great Council.

The Iroquois were hunters, but they had also developed an important agricultural base. Beans, maize and squash were known as the 'three sisters of the Iroquois.'

Samuel de Champlain aided the Huron (Wyandot) in their war against the Iroquois in 1609, which resulted in the Iroquois allying with the Dutch. After receiving firearms from their new European allies, the Iroquois attacked and virtually destroyed the Huron and Erie, and enslaved a large number of Delaware. Having reached the pinnacle of their military power with 3000 men under arms, the Iroquois League extended its area of influence south into Cherokee country. By 1684 they had pushed the Illinois west of the Illinois River.

When the Dutch sold New Amsterdam to the English in 1664, the Iroquois (notably the Mohawks) were quick to make peace with the latter, and in 1710 an Iroquois delegation under King Hendrick (Thoyanoguen) went to England to pay a courtesy call on the court of Queen Anne. Relations continued to be poor with the French, and after 1687 the Iroquois destroyed LaChine and attacked Montreal.

In 1738 William Johnson came to trade with the Iroquois and succeeded in cementing the good relations between them

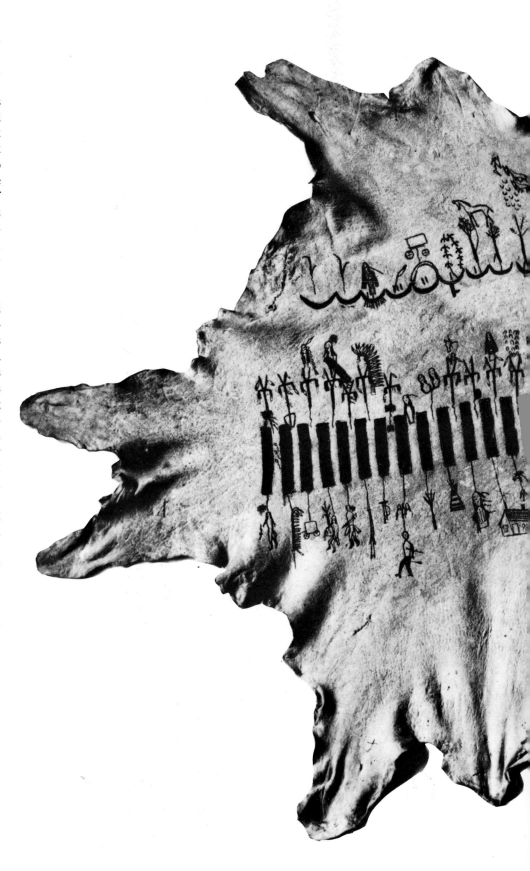

and the English, which survived through the French and Indian War. Johnson led the Mohawks to victory at Lake George in 1755 and at Niagara in 1759. During the American Revolution the British attempted to enlist the aid of the Iroquois and invited Chief Thayendanegea (Joseph Brant) to England in 1775. After his visit to King George, Thayendanegea returned to lead the Mohawks in attacks on Forts Schuyler and Oriskany, as well as in the bloody Cherry Valley Massacre. In 1779, however, General John Sullivan led a counterattack that successfully crippled the power of the Iroquois.

After the defeat of the British and the establishment of the United States, the Americans set aside reservations for the Iroquois in New York State. Many of the Mohawks under Thayendanegea, however, resettled in Canada north of Lake Ontario. The total Iroquois population in Canada was listed as 20,342 in 1967. In 1985 on the New York reservations there were 413 Cayuga, 211 Oneida, 669 Onandaga, 3025 Mohawk and 5548 Seneca. In Oklahoma the combined population of the Seneca and Cayuga was 753, and in Wisconsin the Oneida reservation had a population of 4437.

Isleta Pueblo (*see* Pueblo)

Iswa (*see* Catawba)

Jemez Pueblo (*see* Apache)

Jicarilla Apache (*see* Apache)

John Day
Geographic Region: Great Basin (central Oregon along Columbia River)
Linguistic Group: Penutian-Sahaptin
Principal Dwelling Type: Crude conical tipi
Principal Subsistence Type: Mix of animal and wild plant foods

Juaneño
Geographic Region: Southeastern California
Linguistic Group: Uto-Aztecan
Principal Dwelling Type: Domed bark, thatch or hide house
Principal Subsistence Type: Mix of animal and wild plant foods, maize

The Juaneño were one of the 'mission peoples' tribes who embraced Spanish culture and religion soon after the arrival of the Spaniards. In his 1925 survey, Alfred Kroeber estimated their aboriginal population at about 1000.

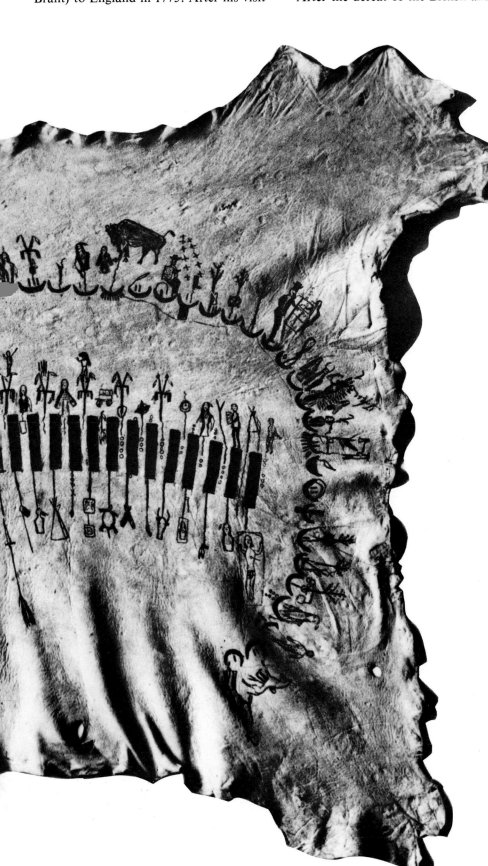

Left: A calendar of 37 months, 1889-92, kept on a buffalo skin by Anko, a Kiowa man who recorded events in simple pictograph form. Such events as a measles epidemic are recorded on this type of calendar, unique among the North American tribes. Since no universal symbols existed, a calendar was difficult to read.

K

Kadohadacho (*see* Caddo)

Kaigani (*see* Haida)

Kake (*see* Tlingit)

Kalapuya (Calapooya)
Geographic Region: Great Basin (Willamette Valley, Oregon)
Linguistic Group: Penutian
Principal Dwelling Type:
Semisubterranean house
Principal Subsistence Type: Mix of animal and wild plant foods

Kalispel (Lower Pend d'Oreille)
Geographic Region: Great Basin (northwestern Montana, Idaho panhandle)
Linguistic Group: Salishan
Principal Dwelling Type:
Semisubterranean house
Principal Subsistence Type: Large game
The traditional range of the Kalispel was near that of the Spokane, with whom they are closely related. The present town of Kalispell, Montana is named for them, even though their range was farther to the north and west. The present Kalispel Reservation in Washington, which had a population of 259 in 1985, is associated with the Spokane Agency.

Kaluschian (*see* Tlingit)

Kamia
Geographic Region:
Southwestern California (San Diego)
Linguistic Group: Hokan-Yuman
Principal Dwelling Type: Domed bark, thatch or hide house
Principal Subsistence Type: Acorns
The Kamia were associated with the Diegueño, and had an aboriginal population of roughly 1000.

Kanianigmiut (North Alaskan Eskimo, *see* Eskimo)

Kansa (Kaw)
Geographic Region: Plains and Prairies
Linguistic Group: Siouan-Dhegiha
Principal Dwelling Type:
Prairie-Southwest earth lodge

Opposite: **A George Catlin portrait of Little Bluff, who led the Kiowas from 1834-64. The Kalapuya tribe fashioned the arrowheads (*above*) and the scrapers and arrowheads (*below*). Of the four points below, the largest is a small game point; the other three are for hunting birds.**

Principal Subsistence Type: Hunting, maize
The Kansa, whose name means 'south wind people,' are related to both the Osage and Omaha. They were observed by Father Jacques Marquette at the mouth of the Kansas River in 1673. In 1846 they were assigned a reservation near Topeka, Kansas, of which half was ceded back to the United States in 1859 and the balance sold between 1872 and 1880. The proceeds were used to buy a new reservation opened in June 1873, in Indian Territory. The initial population of the new Kaw Agency was 533, but it declined to 194 by 1889. Between 1902 and 1906, the Kansa land was divided among the remaining 247 members of the tribe in anticipation of Oklahoma statehood.

There had been approximately 1700 Kansa in 1850 and there were 580 left in Oklahoma in 1950. In 1985 the Kaw tribe at the Pawnee Agency in Oklahoma listed a population of 543.

Karankawa
Geographic Region: Southeast (Texas coast)
Linguistic Group: Coahuiltecan
Principal Dwelling Type: Domed bark, thatch or hide house
Principal Subsistence Type: Fish

Karok
Geographic Region: Northwestern California (Klamath River)
Linguistic Group: Hokan-Karok
Principal Dwelling Type:
Semisubterranean house
Principal Subsistence Type: Mix of animal and wild plant foods
The Karok and the Yurok were the two major tribes of Northern California, and in 1880 their combined population totaled 1125 on the Lower Klamath River Reservation. In 1985 the Karok tribe had a population of 2096, making it the largest Indian group in the state of California.

Kasihta (*see* Creek)

Kaska
Geographic Region: Subarctic (British Columbia, Yukon Territory)
Linguistic Group: Athapascan
Principal Dwelling Type: Crude conical tipi
Principal Subsistence Type:
Caribou, moose

Kaskaskia (*see* Illinois)

Kathlamet (*see* Chinook)

Kato
Geographic Region:
Northwestern California
Linguistic Group: Athapascan
Principal Dwelling Type:
Rectangular plank house
Principal Subsistence Type: Mix of animal and wild plant foods

Kavelchadom
Geographic Region: Southwest (Arizona)
Linguistic Group: Hokan-Yuman

Principal Dwelling Type: Domed bark, thatch or hide house
Principal Subsistence Type: Wild plants, small game

Kaviagmiut (West Alaskan Eskimo, *see* Eskimo)

Kaw (*see* Kansa)

Kawaiisu
Geographic Region: California (central Sierra Nevada)
Linguistic Group: Uto-Aztecan
Principal Dwelling Type: Crude conical tipi
Principal Subsistence Type: Wild plants, small game

Kawchodinneh (*see* Hare)

Kichai (Kitsash, Keechi)
Geographic Region: Plains and Prairies (Texas)
Linguistic Group: Caddoan
Principal Dwelling Type:
Prairie-Southwest earth lodge
Principal Subsistence Type: Maize

The Kichai, whose name means 'red shield,' were first observed by white men in 1701 on the upper reaches of the Trinity and Red rivers in Texas, where they were associated with the Wichita and traded with the Kiowa. In 1842, when Zachary Taylor attended the grand council of the Creek Nation, the Kichai were present. During the Civil War, most of the tribe remained loyal to the Union and moved north into Kansas from their homes on the Washita River in Indian Territory. A majority of the tribe was wiped out in the cholera epidemic of 1867, and the survivors returned to Indian Territory, where they became affiliated with the Wichita and the Wichita-Caddo reservation.

The Kichai population is said to have been 300 in 1849, 52 in 1894 and 30 in 1905, prior to Oklahoma statehood. In 1950 there remained 47 Kichai on the Anadarko Reservation in Oklahoma.

Kickapoo
Geographic Region:
Northeast (Wisconsin)
Linguistic Group: Algonquian
Principal Dwelling Type: Domed bark, thatch or hide house
Principal Subsistence Type:
Hunting, maize

The Kickapoo name derives from Kiwigapawa, meaning 'he moves about, standing now here, now there.' The tribe was recorded in 1667 as living in southern Wisconsin. After the defeat of the Illi-

nois in the French and Indian War, they moved into southern Illinois. They were among the tribes in the confederation formed by Tecumseh from 1811 to 1813, and later joined Black Hawk during the hostilities of the early 1830s. The Kickapoo were signatories of the 1795 Greenville Treaty, and in 1819 they ceded their lands in Illinois to the US government in exchange for a reservation in Missouri, which was in turn ceded in 1832 in exchange for a tiny reservation in Kansas.

Some Kickapoo factions who disagreed with the cessions moved to Texas to join the Cherokee. In 1839 this group was defeated by the Texans and forced onto the Choctaw Nation in Indian Territory, which they in turn abandoned for Mexico in 1850. They did not return until 1873, and it was 1905 before the Mexican Kickapoo were allotted land in Indian Territory.

The Kickapoo population was estimated at 220 in 1825 and only 194 a century later. In 1985 the population of the Kickapoo Reservation in Kansas was 603, while the Mexican Kickapoo tribe numbered 1001 in Oklahoma and 463 in Texas.

Killisnoo (*see* Tlingit)

Kinugmiut (West Alaskan Eskimo, *see* Eskimo)

Kiowa
Geographic Region: Plains and Prairies
Linguistic Group: Uto-Aztecan
Principal Dwelling Type: Plains tipi

Below: Satank or Sitting Bear, a Kiowa Chief whose bloody escape attempt while under arrest ended in his own death on 28 May 1871.

Principal Subsistence Type: Buffalo

The Kiowa name is derived from *kai-gwa,* meaning 'principal people,' and legend has it that they originated in the Yellowstone River country of central Montana. In the eighteenth century, having obtained horses, they moved onto the plains to hunt buffalo. During this time they made alliances with both the Kiowa-Apache as well as their former enemies, the Comanche. This latter association was the basis for the Kiowa-Comanche Reservation formed in Indian Territory in 1892.

The Kiowa are noted for having kept a written history. This historical record was kept in the form of a pictographic calendar painted and updated twice a year, in winter and summer, on buffalo skins. This intricate calendar, unique among the tribes north of Mexico, was actually produced by the tribe annually from 1832 through 1892. From 1893 until his death in 1939, the tradition was kept alive by George Poolaw, a Kiowa. The calendar records such events as the 1877 and 1892 measles epidemics, and set 1879 as the year that the buffalo 'disappeared.' The Ghost Dance craze (*see* Apache and Paiute) is recorded, as is the 1906 statehood of Oklahoma and the sale of Kiowa land to the white man.

The US Government Indian Office recorded that the Kiowa population remained fairly stable during the nineteenth century despite the epidemics of 1877 and 1892. These figures were first recorded in 1875, the year the Kiowa surrendered to the government at Fort Sill, Oklahoma, and subsequently taken at decade intervals for over 40 years. There were 1070 Kiowa in 1875, 1169 in 1885, 1037 in 1895, and 1195 in 1905. The populations of other tribes experienced much greater increases and decreases during those years. In 1970 the population stood at 2692, up from 1699 in 1924. In 1985 there were 3999 members of the Kiowa tribe at the Anadarko Agency in Oklahoma.

Kiowa Apache (*see* Apache)

Kitamat
Geographic Region: Northwest Coast (east-central British Columbia)
Linguistic Group: Algonquian-Wakashan
Principal Dwelling Type:
Semisubterranean house
Principal Subsistence Type: Large game, fish

Kite (Staitan)
Geographic Region: Plains and Prairies (Black Hills)
Linguistic Group: Siouan

Above: **A seated group of Kwakiutl women and children at Quatsino Sound in British Columbia. This 1880 photograph shows the results of their head deformation practice that involved strapping flat planks of wood to the backs of their heads, producing the elongated flattened shape. Another custom was cremation; only the Shaman could be buried.**

Principal Dwelling Type: Plains tipi
Principal Subsistence Type: Hunting

Kititas (Kittitas)
Geographic Region: Great Basin (central Washington)
Linguistic Group: Penutian-Sahaptin
Principal Dwelling Type: Semisubterranean house
Principal Subsistence Type: Large game, fish

Kitkehahki (*see* Pawnee)

Kitsash (*see* Kichai)

Klallam (Clallam)
Geographic Region: Northwest Coast (US side Straits Juan de Fuca)
Linguistic Group: Salishan
Principal Dwelling Type: Rectangular plank house
Principal Subsistence Type: Fish

Klamath
Geographic Region: Great Basin (southern Oregon, Northern California)
Linguistic Group: Lutuamian (similar to Modoc)
Principal Dwelling Type: Semisubterranean house, crude conical tipi
Principal Subsistence Type: Mix of animal and wild plant foods

The Klamath were related to the nearby Modocs and lived a similar lifestyle as hunters and gatherers. Baked grasshoppers were considered a delicacy. They first encountered the white man in 1826, and were visited again during John Charles Fremont's expeditions in 1843 and 1846. They remained at peace with the white man, and in return were generally respected on their reservation, which they were granted in 1864 and shared with 35 other tribes, including the Modoc.

The population of the Lower Klamath Reservation in California varied widely, from 374 in 1868 to 1125 in 1880, to 213 in 1887, to 673 in 1897, to 791 in 1911. Except for 1887, these figures probably include tribes other than the Klamath.

Klasset (*see* Makah)

Klatskanie (Clatskanie)
Geographic Region: Northwest Coast (northern Oregon coast)
Linguistic Group: Salishan
Principal Dwelling Type: Rectangular plank house
Principal Subsistence Type: Fish

Klikitat
Geographic Region: Northwest Coast
Linguistic Group: Penutian-Sahaptin
Principal Dwelling Type: Semisubterranean house
Principal Subsistence Type: Fish

Koasati (Choushatta, Koasota)
Geographic Region: Southeast (Mobile, Alabama)
Linguistic Group: Algonquian

Principal Dwelling Type: Rectangular thatched house
Principal Subsistence Type: Fish

Kobukmiut (North Alaskan Eskimo, *see* Eskimo)

Kogohue (*see* Shoshone)

Kohuana
Geographic Region: Southwest (Arizona)
Linguistic Group: Hokan-Yuman
Principal Dwelling Type: Domed bark, thatch or hide house
Principal Subsistence Type: Wild plants, small game

Kolash (*see* Tlingit)

Kolomi (*see* Creek)

Konkonelp (*see* Okinagan)

Kootenai (Kootenay, Kutenai)
Geographic Region: Great Basin (intersection of Idaho, Montana and British Columbia)
Linguistic Group: Kitunahan (Algonquian)
Principal Dwelling Type: Plains tipi
Principal Subsistence Type: Wild game

An associate of the Spokane tribe, the Kootenai formerly lived east of the Rocky Mountains, but were forced westward by their traditional enemies, the Blackfoot. They now live in a region where their name has been given to a major lake, a river and a Canadian national park. The tribe is divided into upper and lower divisions, the latter being the more primi-

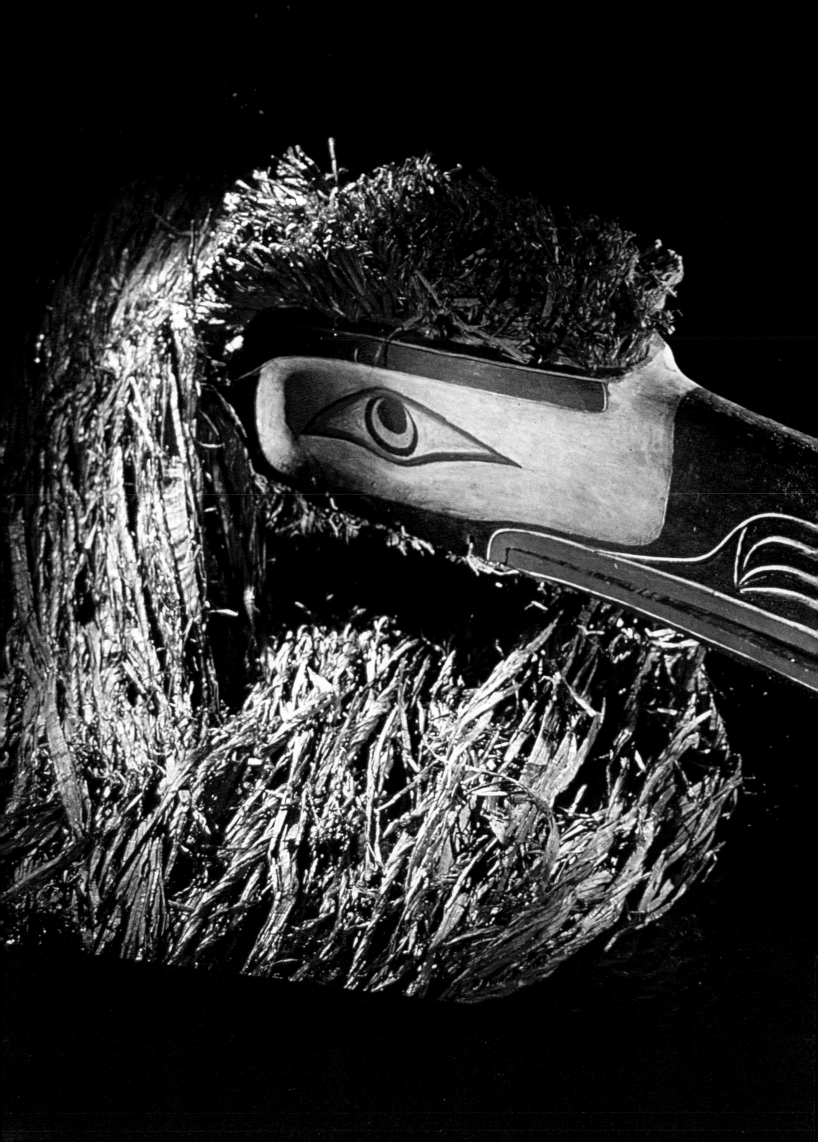

Left: A Kwakiutl raven mask nearly five feet long. In the Hamatsa dance the raven eats the eyes of the Cannibal Dancer's victims. *Right:* An articulated Kwakiutl story-telling mask. The hinged exterior mask was opened at the appropriate moment in the story to reveal the interior mask.

Below: Dancers in the Kwakiutl Winter Ceremony wear carved and polychromed masks of all sizes that represent animals and birds important to their tribe's legends.

tive and nomadic. Relations between the Kootenai and the white man have always been generally good, and relations are presently good with the Blackfoot as well, after years of animosity. In 1967 there were 549 Kootenai on the reservation in Canada, and in 1985 the Kootenai Reservation in Idaho had a population of 123.

Koso (*see* Shoshone)

Koyukon
Geographic Region: Subarctic (Yukon and Kuskokwin rivers, central Alaska)
Linguistic Group: Athapascan
Principal Dwelling Type: Rectangular earth-covered Alaskan house
Principal Subsistence Type:
Caribou, moose, fish

Kugmiut (North Alaskan Eskimo, *see* Eskimo)

Kuiu (*see* Tlingit)

Kutchin
Geographic Region: Subarctic (coastal mountains, Alaska and British Columbia)
Linguistic Group: Athapascan
Principal Dwelling Type:
Double lean-to
Principal Subsistence Type:
Caribou, moose, fish

Kutenai (*see* Kootenai)

Kwakiutl
Geographic Region: Northwest Coast (central British Columbia coast)
Linguistic Group:
Algonquian-Wakashan
Principal Dwelling Type:
Rectangular plank house
Principal Subsistence Type: Fish

The Kwakiutl were one of the major tribes of the Northwest Coast and once encompassed other nearby tribes such as the Bella Bella, Kitimat, Makah and Nootka, with whom they are linguistically related. Their villages were typical of the Northwest Coast, with large cedar plank houses and intricately carved totem poles, representing the animals with whom a particular family might be religiously associated. The Kwakiutl were good traders and welcomed the white man as a trading partner, although contact was sporadic before the mid-nineteenth century. When the anthropologist Franz Boas came to study the Kwakiutl in 1896, their pragmatic chief asked him:

Do you see these woods? Do you see these trees? We shall cut them

Opposite: An 1899 totem pole served as a 'family crest' for the Kwakiutl family who lived in the house behind it. No other clans could use the same combination of animal symbols in their totem pole. *Above:* Guests leave a Kwakiutl potlatch, an elaborate party and often an ostentatious display of wealth. Hosts might burn personal posessions to indicate that they could be easily replaced.

down and build new houses and live as our fathers did. We will dance when our laws command us to dance, we will feast when our hearts command us to feast. Do we ask the white man 'Do as the Indian does?' No, we do not. Why then do you ask us 'Do as the white man does?' It is a strict law that bids us dance. It is a strict law that bids us distribute our property among our friends and neighbors. It is a good law. Let the white man observe his law, we shall observe ours. And now if you are come to forbid us, begone, if not, you will be welcome to us.

In his comments, which were really addressed to all white men rather than just Boas, the chief was careful to mention the 'strict law that bids us to distribute our property among our friends and relatives.' This was a reference to the potlatch ceremony, which the Canadian government was determined to eradicate from Northwest Coast Indian life, and for which Boas supported the Indians.

The potlatch had been the focal point of Northwest Coast cultural life. It was part social, part religious and usually quite political. The ceremony was, in essence, a huge party to which a host would invite guests for as many as 10 days of singing, dancing and feasting. During that time. the host would demonstrate his wealth and success by giving gifts to his guests, even to the verge of bankrupting himself. The more he gave away and the longer the potlatch lasted, the more successful it was. Despite the obvious costs, a successful potlatch would greatly enhance an individual's standing among the members of the tribe.

The potlatch ceremony was officially banned by the Canadian government in 1884, but the 1920s were the peak years of enforcement—in 1921–22 alone 34 Kwakiutl were tried and convicted. In 1951, however, all mention of the potlatch was stricken from the criminal code. A total of 2593 Kwakiutl were recorded living on the Canadian reservation in 1967.

Kwalhioqua

Geographic Region: Great Basin (southern Washington Cascades)
Linguistic Group: Athapascan
Principal Dwelling Type:
    Rectangular plank house
Principal Subsistence Type: Fish, game

Above: **Hamasoka, principal chief of a Kwakiutl village, wearing a blanket decorated with mother of pearl buttons that indicate his staus. The buttons were acquired through trade, an economic system common among Northwestern tribes.** *Opposite top:* **A whale is pulled ashore by a boatload of Makah men at Neah Bay, Washington. The whale is floated with inflated sealskin buoys.**

Labrador Eskimo (*see Eskimo*)

Laguna Pueblo (*see* Pueblo)

Lake
Geographic Region: Great Basin (southern British Columbia)
Linguistic Group: Salishan
Principal Dwelling Type:
  Semisubterranean house
Principal Subsistence Type: Fish, large game

Lake Miwok (*see* Miwok)

Lakota (*see* Sioux)

Lemhi (*see* Shoshone)

Lenni-Lenape (*see* Delaware)

Lillooet
Geographic Region: Great Basin (southern British Columbia)
Linguistic Group: Salishan
Principal Dwelling Type:
  Semisubterranean house
Principal Subsistence Type: Fish, large game
  Related to the Salishan-speaking people of the Northwest Coast, the Lillooet are today one of the largest tribes in western Canada, numbering 2374 in 1967.

Lipan Apache (*see* Apache)

Little Osage (*see* Osage)

Lower Pend d'Oreille (*see* Kalispel)

Luiseño
Geographic Region:
  Southeastern California
Linguistic Group: Uto-Aztecan
Principal Dwelling Type: Domed bark, thatch or hide house
Principal Subsistence Type:
  Acorns, maize
  Known as one of the 'mission peoples' tribes, the Luiseño were also one of the largest tribes in the southern part of California at the time of the arrival of the Spanish. Alfred Kroeber, in his 1925 survey, estimated their aboriginal popula-

tion at 4000. Their 1970 population was 888 on nine Southern California reservations. In 1985 there were 280 people at the La Jolla Reservation, 18 at the La Posta Reservation, 208 at the Los Coyotes Reservation, 28 at the Mesa Grande Reservation, 548 at the Pala Reservation, 107 at the Pauma Yuima Reservation, 637 at the Pechanga Reservation, 427 at the Rincon Reservation, and 486 at the San Pasqual Reservation.

Lumbee

Geographic Region: Southeast (North Carolina)
Linguistic Group: Siouan
Principal Dwelling Type:
   Rectangular barrel-roofed house
Principal Subsistence Type: Maize
Note: Name derived from Lumber River

Lummi

Geographic Region: Northwest Coast (Puget Sound)
Linguistic Group: Salishan
Principal Dwelling Type: Rectangular plank house, semisubterranean house
Principal Subsistence Type: Fish

In 1985 the Lummi Reservation had a population of 2503, making it the second largest reservation (after the Puyallup) in western Washington State.

Mackenzie Eskimo (*see* Eskimo)

Mahican

Geographic Region: Northeast
Linguistic Group: Algonquian
Principal Dwelling Type:
   Rectangular barrel-roofed house
Principal Subsistence Type: Maize, fish
Subgroup: Wawyachtonoc and possibly Wea

The Mahican, made famous in James Fenimore Cooper's book *Last of the Mohicans,* are not to be confused with the Mohegan, who are *correctly* referred to as Mohican.

The Mahican were an Algonquian tribe of five groups living in the Hudson River valley of upper New York State, and hence were also called the River Indian. They were allied to the Munsee and Delaware. *(See also* Wea)

Maidu

Geographic Region: California (Central Valley)
Linguistic Group: Penutian-Maidu
Principal Dwelling Type:
   Semisubterranean house
Principal Subsistence Type: Acorns
Subgroups: Maidu Proper, Nishinam (Nisenan)

The Maidu were originally referred to as the 'Digger' Indians because they dug for edible roots. Their main food source, as with most other California tribes, was the acorn, which was ground into flour for making bread.

Prior to the arrival of the white man, the Maidu were one of the largest tribes in California and, indeed, in all of North America. The aboriginal Maidu and Nishinam population was estimated in Sherburne Cook's 1955 survey to include 47,000 people in the Sacramento River valley, and 8450 in the Sierra Nevada foothills. The population density was estimated at between 2.4 and 3.4 persons per square mile in the valley and foothills. In 1985 the population of the Enterprise Rancheria near Oroville, California was 338.

Makah (Klasset, Makaw, Micaw)

Geographic Region: Northwest Coast

Linguistic Group: Wakashan
Principal Dwelling Type:
Rectangular plank house
Principal Subsistence Type: Fish

The Makah, whose name means 'cape people,' are located in the Cape Flattery area of Washington near the Hoko River and Tatoosh Island. They are the southernmost of the Wakashan peoples and are related to the Nootka. They ceded much of their land to the US government in 1855, and were consolidated onto a small reservation in 1893. After World War II, the Makah purchased an abandoned US Army engineer's camp at Neah Bay, where they established their reservation. In 1985 the population of the Makah Reservation was 919.

Malecite (Maliseet)
Geographic Region: Northeast (New Brunswick, Maine)
Linguistic Group: Algonquian
Principal Dwelling Type: Crude conical tipi
Principal Subsistence Type: Caribou, moose, fish

The Malecite have been traditionally associated with the Abnaki, Passamaquoddy and Penobscot tribes. In 1967 there were 1626 Malecite in Canada. In 1982 the Houlton band of Maliseet Indians in Maine numbered 245. *(See also Abnaki)*

Malemiut (West Alaskan Eskimo, *see* Eskimo)

Maliseet (*see* Malecite)

Mandan
Geographic Region: Plains and Prairies (Missouri River, central North Dakota)
Linguistic Group: Siouan
Principal Dwelling Type: Large circular earthen lodges
Principal Subsistence Type:
Hunting, maize, pumpkins, squash

Unlike the other tribes on the great plains, the Mandan were sedentary peoples, living in lodges in large villages along the upper Missouri River. Slant Village in North Dakota, occupied in the late eighteenth century, shows traces of 75 lodges, including the large ceremonial lodge that is 84 feet in diameter. Also unlike other

Right: **Like other Plains Indians, the Mandan tribe performed buffalo dances to ensure a steady supply of meat and hides. In this painting by George Catlin, dancers wear skins and imitate the animal's movements in an attempt to bring its spirit closer to the tribe's hunting range. In addition to providing meat, the animal supplied skin for clothing, bones for tools and entrails for cooking pouches.**

Plains tribes, the Mandan made pottery.

The Mandan were associated with the Hidatsa and Arikara, and their first contact with the white man was in 1738. They were visited in 1804 by Lewis and Clark and in 1833 by George Catlin, whose paintings preserve much of what we know about the Mandan. In 1837 a smallpox epidemic devastated the tribe, reducing its population from over 1800 persons to 23 men, 40 women, and roughly 65 children. In 1970 the Mandan population of the Fort Berthold Reservation in North Dakota stood at 705.

Maricopa
Geographic Region: Southwest (southeastern California)
Linguistic Group: Hokan-Yuman
Principal Dwelling Type: Domed bark, thatch or hide house
Principal Subsistence Type: Wild plants, maize

Mascouten
Geographic Region: Plains and Prairies
Linguistic Group: Algonquian
Principal Dwelling Type: Plains tipi
Principal Subsistence Type: Mix of hunting and wild plants

Massachuset
Geographic Region:
Northeast (Massachusetts)
Linguistic Group: Algonquian
Principal Dwelling Type:
Rectangular barrel-roofed house
Principal Subsistence Type:
Hunting, maize

The name Massachuset derives from the Algonquian word that means 'near the great hills.' The tribal name was adopted for the English colony and later for the state of Massachusetts.

Mattapony
Geographic Region: Northeast
Linguistic Group: Algonquian
Principal Dwelling Type:
Rectangular barrel-roofed house
Principal Subsistence Type: Maize

Mattole
Geographic Region:
Northwestern California
Linguistic Group: Athapascan
Principal Dwelling Type:
Rectangular plank house
Principal Subsistence Type: Mix of animal and wild plant foods

Maumee (*see* Miami)

Mayucas (*see* Seminole)

M'dewakanton (*see* Sioux)

Meherrin (*see* Susquehannock)

Menominee
Geographic Region: Northeast (northern Wisconsin)
Linguistic Group: Algonquian
Principal Dwelling Type: Domed bark, thatch or hide house
Principal Subsistence Type: Mix of animal and wild plant foods, especially wild rice

The Menominee, whose name signifies 'wild rice,' have never ranged far from the site of their present reservation near Wolf Lake in Wisconsin, where they harvested but did not plant wild rice because their religion forbade agriculture. They are more closely related to the Sauk, Fox and Kickapoo than to the neighboring Chippewa and Ottawa. Their first contact with the white man was with Jean Nicolet in 1634, and they remained allied with the French until 1763, after the French and Indian War. They supported the English in the War of 1812 and have lived on the reservation since 1831. In 1985 the reservation population was 3582, up from 3570 in 1970.

Mescalero Apache (*see* Apache)

Mesquaki (*see* Fox)

Methow
Geographic Region: Northwest Coast (north-central Washington)
Linguistic Group: Salishan
Principal Dwelling Type:
Rectangular plank house
Principal Subsistence Type: Fish

Miami (Maumee, Twightwee)
Geographic Region: Northeast (Illinois and Wisconsin)
Linguistic Group: Algonquian
Principal Dwelling Type: Domed bark, thatch or hide house
Principal Subsistence Type: Maize
Subgroups: Piankashaw, Peoria (Piware, Peouaria), Eel River

The Miami, whose name comes from the Chippewa *omaumeg,* or 'people who live on the peninsula,' first came into contact with white men in 1658 near Green Bay, Wisconsin, but they soon withdrew to the headwaters of the Fox River and later to the headwaters of the Wabash and Maumee rivers. The Miami had good relations with the French, with whom they were allied. They were also closely associated with the Piankashaw, who were once thought to be part of the Miami tribe.

The Miami took part in Pontiac's uprising, and under Chief Little Turtle (1747-1812) they defeated General Josiah Harmer twice in 1790 and General Arthur St Clair in 1791. In 1794 they were defeated by General 'Mad' Anthony Wayne at the Battle of Fallen Timbers. In the subsequent Greenville Treaty they ceded all of southern and eastern Ohio to the US government. During the War of 1812, they joined Tecumseh and the Shawnee in support of the British. They were defeated, however, by Colonel John Campbell in the Battle of Mississinewa on 18 December 1812. In 1838 most of the Miami were removed to Kansas, and in 1867 some of the Miami in Kansas confederated with other tribes and moved to Indian Territory. In 1873 the remaining Miami joined the Peoria in Indian Territory. The 1985 Miami tribe population in Oklahoma numbered 393, up from 323 in 1970.

Micai
Geographic Region: Northwest Coast (central Washington)
Linguistic Group: Sahaptin
Principal Dwelling Type:
Rectangular plank house
Principal Subsistence Type: Fish

Micaw (*see* Makah)

Miccosukee (Mikasuki, *see* Seminole)

Michigamea (*see* Illinois)

Micmac (Mikwak, Mikwanak)
Geographic Region: Northeast (Canadian Maritimes, northern Maine)
Linguistic Group: Algonquian
Principal Dwelling Type: Crude conical tipi
Principal Subsistence Type:
Caribou, moose, fish

The original home of the Micmac was southern and eastern Newfoundland, Prince Edward Island, Nova Scotia, Cape Breton and northern New Brunswick. This area was near the lands of the Abnaki, to whom the Micmac were not related.

The Micmac may have been the first Indians north of the Caribbean to en-

Above left: **Dan Waupoose, a Menominee chief, photographed in 1943 wearing his feathered headdress.** *Far left:* **Michikinikwa ('Little Turtle'), chief of the Miami tribe. He led several attacks against American forces in the Seminole Wars, most of which were successful.** *Left:* **A Micmac camp at Dartmouth, Nova Scotia, 1860. The tipi behind the man and boy is made of birchbark. This material was valued for its strength, flexibility and water-resistant surface.**

Far left: **The Mandan's** *o-kee-pa* **rites emphasized placating the spirits of nature and ended with torture tests to determine new leaders. Two men hang from pegs skewered under their skin. Afterward, the masked warrior at right would chop off a finger.** *Above:* **The Mandan chief Four Bears. This painting, like the other two, are by George Catlin.** *Below:* **O-kee-pa dancers, representing night and day, perform the Mandan creation myth of light replacing darkness during the birth of the world.**

Below: Every medicine man owned a bundle of tools and supplies that he used to cure illnesses. These items belonged to Thomas Smith, the Miwok singing doctor from Bodega Bay, California, who is pictured on the facing page at lower left. Included are the animal skins worn during the curing ritual, a cane whistle, pouches for carrying herbs, mortar and pestles for grinding and mixing medicines, an embroidered moccasin paint bag, obsidian knife blades, feathers, and a rattle.

counter Europeans. Members of the tribe are said to have gone to Europe with Henry Cabot in 1497. Having made early contact with the French, the Micmac remained hostile to the English until after the French and Indian War. Between 1611 and 1760, the estimated Micmac population remained in the 3000 to 3500 range. In 1880 there were between 3800 and 4000, and in 1967 the Micmac population stood at 8645.

Mikasuki (*see* Seminole)

Mikwak, Mikwanak (*see* Micmac)

Minneconjou Sioux (*see* Sioux)

'Mission peoples tribes' (*see* Cahuilla, Cupeño, Diegueño, Fernandeño, Gabrileño, Juaneño, Luiseño and Serraño)

Missouri
Geographic Region: Plains and Prairies
Linguistic Group: Siouan-Chiewere
Principal Dwelling Type: Domed bark, thatch or hide house
Principal Subsistence Type: Hunting, maize
(See also Oto)

Miwok
Geographic Region: California
Linguistic Group: Penutian-Miwok
Principal Dwelling Type: Crude conical tipi
Principal Subsistence Type: Acorns
Subgroups: Coast Miwok, Lake Miwok
The Miwok inhabited the area from the Pacific Coast just north of San Francisco Bay to present-day Yosemite National Park. In his 1956 survey, Sherburne Cook estimated an aboriginal Miwok population of over 19,000. In 1985 there were 280 Miwok living on two rancheria in the Sierra Nevada foothills, up from a total tribal population of 130 in 1970. A Coast Miwok village, including acorn graineries and a large sweat lodge, has been reconstructed to original specifications at the Point Reyes National Seashore north of San Francisco.

Modoc
Geographic Region: California (California and Oregon border)
Linguistic Group: Lutuamian (similar to Klamath)
Principal Dwelling Type: Semisubterranean house
Principal Subsistence Type: Mix of animal and wild plant foods
The Modoc were culturally more close-

Above: **Modoc Woman Sub-Chief Winema (Woman of the Brave Heart), 1873. When settlers petitioned the government to force the Modocs back onto the Klamath Reservation, she attended the council between the Modocs and Captain James Jackson as an interpreter,** requesting peaceful relations. *Below right:* **Kientpoos ('Captain Jack'), chief of the Modocs, who was urged into war by antagonistic whites and members of his own tribe. After Canby was shot, Kientpoos was hunted down and hanged at Fort Klamath.**

Opposite: **Baskets typical of those made by the California tribes. Most were made of sedge root, willow, bullrush root, and redbud bark and held nuts, fish and berries.** *Left:* **A Modoc headdress. A chief's esteem was represented by the size and number of feathers in his headdress.** *Below left:* **Beaded Modoc slippers made of hide.**

mained for five years before briefly returning to the reservation in 1869.

Trouble between the Klamaths and Modocs ensued, and Captain Jack once again led his people back to the old Modoc country along California's Lost River. When they refused a 26 November 1872 government order to return to the reservation, the US Army was ordered to use a show of force to compel their obedience. On 29 November about 30 troopers approached the Modocs, most of whom put down their weapons peaceably. Scarfaced Charlie was a bit reluctant to do so, and when an officer attempted to coerce him it proved a fatal mistake. The ensuing firefight developed into what became known as the Modoc War, or the Lava Beds Campaign, after the volcanic badlands into which Captain Jack and his approximately 80 warriors withdrew.

By spring Captain Jack was surrounded and a meeting was set up in an attempt to negotiate a peaceful settlement. However, a disagreement ensued in which General E R S Canby fell victim to a bullet from Captain Jack's gun, and in which Bogus Charlie killed Sir Eleazer Thomas as he was attempting to escape after being wounded by another Modoc, Boston Charlie. Within moments, other troopers reached the council tent only to find the two men dead, another wounded and the Indians gone. In their attempts to catch the Indians in the labyrinth that was the Lava Beds, the Army took heavy casualties during the ensuing weeks. Over time, discord developed in the Modoc camp and caused some of the Indians, including Bogus Charlie, to turn sides. After having been surrounded twice and having lost many of his best men to Army bullets or desertion, Captain Jack surrendered. Six Modocs were arraigned for murder and four, including Jack, were hanged at Fort Klamath on 3 October 1873 in front of 500 Klamath Indians. The remainder of the Modoc tribe, then numbering 247 and including Bogus Charlie, were sent to a tiny plot of land in Indian Territory, and a few of the very worst offenders were sent to Fort Marion, Florida, where it is reported that they converted to Christianity.

In 1864 the Modoc were estimated to have had a population of about 700. In 1890 there were 84 Modoc in Indian Terri-

ly related to the Indians of the Great Basin than of California. An exception was the Klamath, with whom they shared a common linguistic group, and it was to the Klamath reservation that the Modoc were assigned when their land was ceded to the US government in 1864. Bad feelings between whites and Modocs ran deeper than between whites and any other California tribe, dating back to the 1852 massacre of 75 whites at Tule Lake. Ben

Wright of Yreka had put together a vigilante posse and lured 46 prominent Modocs to a proposed peace talk that resulted in the death of 41 of them. Wright was rewarded with the post of Indian agent and the bad feelings became ingrained on both sides as a result. Shortly after the signing of the 1864 treaty, a large number of Modocs under Kientepoos (Captain Jack) left the reservation for their former home, where they re-

tory and 151 on the Klamath Reservation in Oregon. In 1905 the respective populations were 56 and 223. In 1985 the Modoc Tribe in Oklahoma had a population of 133.

Mohave (*see* Mojave)

Mohawk (*see* Iroquois)

Mohegan (Mohican)
Geographic Region:
   Northeast (Connecticut)
Linguistic Group: Algonquian
Principal Dwelling Type:
   Rectangular barrel-roofed house
Principal Subsistence Type: Fish
   The Mohegan are not to be confused with the Mahican, who were the subject of James Fenimore Cooper's book *The Last of the Mohicans.* The Mohegans were probably once part of the Pequot tribe and lived near them into the seventeenth century. In 1637 Uncas, a sachem banished by the Pequots, became chief of the Mohegans and led 70 warriors under Captain John Mason's New England troops to massacre 600 Pequots at Fort Mystic. In the 1643 to 1945 period, Uncas

Above: **Members of the Klamath, Modoc and Paiute tribes drove to a 1929 tribal council on the Klamath Reservation in Beatty, Oregon, in their Model As.** *Below:* **Scarfaced Charley was a member of the Modoc tribe under Captain Jack. His scar made him fierce-looking, but he supported his chief's policy of peace. In 1873, the Modocs were defeated and sent to the Quapaw Reservation. After Captain Jack was hanged, Scarfaced Charley took over as tribal leader.**

was backed by the state of Massachusetts in wars with the Narragansetts, who were favored by Rhode Island. A land grant made by Uncas in 1640 remained in litigation through 1773, but the Mohegans were assigned a small reservation in New London County, Connecticut.

Moingwena (*see* Illinois)

Mojave (Mohave)
Geographic Region:
   Southeastern California
Linguistic Group: Hokan-Yuman
Principal Dwelling Type: Mojave-type
   four-pitch-roof house
Principal Substance Type: Wild and cultivated plants
   The Mojave were the most populous and warlike of the Yuman-speaking tribes, having had an estimated 1834 population of 4000. They traditionally lived on both sides of the lower Colorado River in the area of the Mojave Desert, where they raised corn, pumpkins, melons and beans, and gathered mesquite beans and pine nuts, but did very little hunting. The Mojave made trouble for immigrants passing through the region, but were in-

volved in no major wars. In 1865 they were placed on the Colorado River Reservation on the Arizona-California border, along with the Chemehuevi. In 1905 the Mojave there numbered 1589. In 1985 there were 2151 people on the Colorado River Reservation (98 percent of them in Arizona), and 503 people on the nearby Fort Mojave Reservation (63 percent of them in California).

Molale (Molalla)
Geographic Region: Great Basin (north-central Oregon)
Linguistic Group: Penutian-Sahaptin
Principal Dwelling Type: Crude conical tipi
Principal Subsistence Type: Mix of animal and wild plant foods

Mono (*see* Paiute)

Montagnais
Geographic Region: Subarctic (Labrador)
Linguistic Group: Algonquian Principal
Dwelling Type: Crude conical tipi
Principal Subsistence Type: Wild game, fish

The Montagnais were traditionally re-lated to the Naskapi and the Abnaki of Maine. They developed splint basketry at the end of the nineteenth century, which replaced their traditional use of birch bark containers. They occasionally fought with the Eskimo, but there is no record of any open warfare with any linguistically related peoples. In 1967 there were 5268 Montagnais in Canada.

Montauk
Geographic Region: Northeast (Long Island, New York)
Linguistic Group: Algonquian
Principal Dwelling Type: Rectangular barrel-roofed house
Principal Subsistence Type: Fish

Devastated by war and disease during the seventeenth century, the tribe had all but disappeared by the middle of the nineteenth century. Their name, however, lives on as a town and rocky point, located at the eastern tip of Long Island.

Moor (*see* Delaware)

Mountain
Geographic Region: Subarctic (Alaska and British Columbia mountains)
Linguistic Group: Athapascan
Principal Dwelling Type: Double lean-to
Principal Subsistence Type: Caribou, moose

Muckleshoot
Geographic Region: Northwest Coast (Puget Sound, Washington)
Linguistic Group: Salishan
Principal Dwelling Type: Rectangular plank house
Principal Subsistence Type: Fish

In 1970 there were 2392 people on the Muckleshoot Reservation in Washington State.

Multnomah
Geographic Region: Great Basin (Columbia River, north-central Oregon)
Linguistic Group: Penutian-Chinook
Principal Dwelling Type: Semisubterranean house
Principal Subsistence Type: Fish

Munsee (*see* Delaware)

Muskoke (*see* Creek)

Muskwaki (*see* Fox)

Below: A Navajo sheepherder watches over his flock in Monument Valley, on the Arizona/Utah border. The Spanish brought domesticated sheep to North America during their invasions, and the Navajo acquired their own by raiding Spanish herds. Originally, women owned the flocks, but the men have assumed the role of shepherd. The Navajo Reservation (which completely surrounds the Hopi Reservation) is the largest in the continental United States and joins four states: Arizona, Utah, Colorado and New Mexico.

Left: **A Navajo man and woman appreciate the beauty of their land. Because of its arches and pinnacles, Monument Valley is referred to as the 'Eighth Wonder of the World.'** *Above:* **This man wears the turquoise necklace, earrings and headband traditional of the Navajo.** *Opposite:* **Cottage industry is an economic mainstay on the reservation. Outside their hogan, Navajo women card the wool (*foreground*), spin the yarn (*right*), and weave it into a rug (*background*).**

Nabesna (*see* Tanana)

Nadako (*see* Anadarko)

Nakota (*see* Dakota)

Nambe Pueblo (*see* Pueblo)

Nanticoke (*see* Delaware)

Narragansett

Geographic Region: Northeast (Rhode Island)
Linguistic Group: Algonquian
Principal Dwelling Type:
  Rectangular barrel-roofed house
Principal Subsistence Type: Fish, maize

The Narragansetts resided on the western shore of Narragansett Bay, Rhode Island but dominated other tribes from southern Massachusetts to Long Island. Due in part to the efforts of Roger Williams, who established a settlement in their territory (which later became the city of Providence), they had good relations with the English. The Narragansetts stayed neutral in the 1637 Pequot War and even welcomed some of the few surviving Pequots into their own tribe. The Narragansetts joined the Wamponoag in King Philip's War and suffered almost complete destruction in the Great Swamp Fight on 19 December 1675. Some were dispersed and some remained near Charleston, Rhode Island. In 1950 they were given the right to vote in state elections.

Naskapi

Geographic Region: Subarctic (Davis Inlet, Labrador)
Linguistic Group: Algonquian
Principal Dwelling Type: Crude conical tipi
Principal Subsistence Type: Wild game, fish

The Naskapi were traditionally associated with the much larger Montagnais tribe, who also lived on the Labrador peninsula. In 1967 there were 284 Naskapi remaining in Canada.

Natakmiut (North Alaskan Eskimo, *see* Eskimo)

Natchez

Geographic Region: Southeast (lower Mississippi valley)
Linguistic Group: Hokan-Natchez
Principal Dwelling Type:
  Rectangular thatched house
Principal Subsistence Type: Maize

The name Natchez is derived from the Choctaw words *nakni sakti chaha* that mean 'warriors of the high bluff,' a reference to Natchez Bluff overlooking the Mississippi at the present-day city of Natchez. The name was originally applied to the Indians of this specific region, but ultimately it was extended to cover other nearby tribes and settlements conquered by the Natchez. The original tribe lived in nine towns and had a combined population of about 6000 in the early eighteenth century. They were a sedentary people with a well-developed chieftainship and hierarchy. Their religion involved worshipping the sun and killing the wives of a chief upon his death.

Mistreated by the French, the Natchez revolted in 1720 and were badly defeated in 1723. They rose up again in 1728, massacring 200 Frenchmen in 1729 before being completely defeated in 1730. Afterward, nearly 450 were sold into slavery in the West Indies, while the remainder dispersed among other tribes, especially the Chickasaw.

Nauset

Geographic Region: Northeast (south of Cape Cod)
Linguistic Group: Algonquian

Principal Dwelling Type:
  Rectangular barrel-roofed house
Principal Subsistence Type: Fish

Navajo (Dineh, Navaho)
Geographic Region: Southwest
Linguistic Group: Athapaskan (southern
  group)
Principal Dwelling Type:
  Rectangular wooden house (hogan)
Principal Subsistence Type: Maize, wild
  plants, small game

Traditionally one of the largest tribes in the southwestern United States, the Navajo today occupy a reservation comprising 16 million acres in the Southwest that is larger than several eastern states. The word Navajo derives from the Spanish word for 'people with big fields.' At the time of the arrival of the white man they had developed agriculture, though on a smaller scale than the nearby Hopi and Pueblo peoples. The Navajo were less sedentary than the Hopi and Pueblo tribes, but more so than the Apache of the same region.

With the arrival of the Spanish, the Navajo acquired sheep, which continue to be an important component of their lifestyle. At war constantly with the Spanish, who sought to enslave them, the Navajo withdrew into the mountains and eventually turned Canyon de Chelly in northeastern Arizona into a major stronghold. The Spanish, and later the Americans, raided this stronghold from time to time, but it remained a formidable defensive position until well into the nineteenth century.

The treaty relationship between the United States and the Navajo began in 1846 after the US Army occupation of Santa Fe, but Colonel Alexander Doniphan was not able to obtain the signatures of all the Navajo chiefs. Warfare continued because the authority of each chief extended only to a particular village. Colonel E R S Canby concluded a treaty with 22 of the tribe's chiefs.

In 1863 Colonel Christopher 'Kit' Carson raided Canyon de Chelly, defeating the Navajo and taking them into custody as prisoners of war. They were held for five years at the Bosque Redondo Reservation in eastern New Mexico along with their rivals, the Mescalero Apache. In 1868 a new treaty was signed and the Navajo were permitted to return to Canyon de Chelly. The treaty also provided replacement of the sheep and goats killed in Carson's roundup of the Navajo in 1863. The Navajo have remained at peace with the United States ever since and to this day no one is permitted to enter Canyon de Chelly, now a US national monument, without permission of the Navajo Nation.

The specific boundaries of the Navajo Nation have changed many times over the years, particularly in relation to the Hopi reservation, which it surrounds. Nevertheless, their territory has always been in the northeast corner of Arizona, with additional land in Utah and New Mexico. The center of Navajo government is located at Window Rock, Arizona, about half way between Canyon de Chelly and Gallup, New Mexico. The Navajo Nation contains an area smaller than the original tribal lands, but it is still the largest reservation in the United States. Larger than New Jersey, Connecticut and Massachusetts combined, the Navajo Nation is treated by some federal agencies as a separate state.

During World War II, 3000 Navajo served in the armed service. Notable among these were the 'Navajo code talkers' of the US Marine Corps, who handled radio transmission of classified data. They were able to transmit secret information directly by speaking in their own native language, a code the enemy was never able to break.

Between 1868 and 1900, the Navajo population jumped from about 8000 to almost 20,000, and by 1930 it had doubled to over 40,000. In 1947 there were 61,000 Navajo, and in 1969 the population stood at 122,316. In 1985 there were 166,665 people on the Navajo Nation, 59 percent of them in the Arizona portion of the

Above: A Navajo silversmith hammers silver outside his earth lodge. The small boy, his son, stands by the bellows while the man at right uses a bow drill. This photo was taken in New Mexico about 1893. Modern silversmiths tend to use present-day techniques. *Below right:* Modern Navajo women still weave blankets using the methods used by their ancestors to make the likes of this tightly woven 'Chief Blanket' (*below left*), which displays a characteristic matched design. Navajo handicraft reached a peak during the 'classic period' around 1860. *Opposite:* A woman making bread from corn meal, using a traditional stone oven.

Above: **Medicine Man Charlie Turquoise (in white headwrap) leads a group of Navajo dancers at Fort Wingate, New Mexico, in 1941.** *Right:* **Manuelito, a Navajo chief, was the last to surrender after the Navajo War in 1866.** *Opposite:* **A silversmith displays his tools (***right***) and his work. The Navajos learned the art from the Mexicans. Jewelry was made from Mexican or American currency until sheets of the metal became available.**

reservation, 39 percent in New Mexico and the rest in Utah.

N'de (*see* Apache)

Nespelem
Geographic Region: Great Basin (eastern Washington, western Idaho)
Linguistic Group: Salishan
Principal Dwelling Type: Semisubterranean house
Principal Subsistence Type: Fish, game

Netsilik Eskimo (*see* Eskimo)

Neutral
Geographic Region: Northeast (southern Great Lakes country)
Linguistic Group: Iroquoian
Principal Dwelling Type: Domed bark, thatch or hide house
Principal Subsistence Type: Maize

Nez Percé (Sahaptini)
Geographic Region: Great Basin (Idaho, Oregon, Washington)
Linguistic Group: Sahaptin (Penutian)
Principal Dwelling Type: Plains tipi
Principal Subsistence Type: Large game

The name Nez Percé was given to the Sahaptini because, when they were first encountered by the French, some members of the tribe were seen wearing pendants attached to their pierced noses. They traditionally hunted wild game, especially buffalo, but fished for salmon as well. The Nez Percé had generally good relations with the white man beginning with the French and with Americans such as Lewis and Clark. In 1831 they sent emissaries to St Louis *requesting* Christian missionaries.

The Nez Percé remained neutral in all the region's Indian wars, including the Rogue River Wars of the 1850s. When war clouds next rolled across the valleys and forests of the Northwest, the Nez Percé would write one of the greatest epics in the history of the Indian Wars, and would see the rise to national prominence of one of the greatest Indian leaders of all time. The tribe was actually two tribes, an Upper and Lower Nez Percé, with each occupying its own distinct lands but sharing certain common hunting grounds. This distinction, however, was lost on the US government, who in 1863 signed a treaty with the Upper Nez Percé, who in turn signed away the lands of both Nez Percé groups and moved to the Lapwai Reservation.

It took over 10 years before white population growth in Lower Nez Percé territory reached a level where it encroached on the Indians who still were not abiding by the treaty that had been signed for them. Though local white sentiment actually supported creation of a Lower Nez Percé reservation at Wallowa, Congress declined to approve it. Despite the efforts of the diplomatic mission-school-educated Chief Joseph, the southern wing of the tribe was compelled in 1877 to move from the Wallowa Valley onto the Lapwai Reservation, where natural friction developed between the two groups of Indians. Joseph wanted to avoid bloodshed, but members of his Lower Nez Percé went to war, incurring the wrath of the US Army. General Oliver Otis Howard and Chief Joseph knew and respected one another, but the actions of a few had escalated the violence to a point where it couldn't be turned back. Joseph took command and moved his forces to White Bird Canyon, where on 17 June 1877 they defeated the US Army in the first pitched battle of

Left: **Nez Perce Chief Joseph, in 1877. He avoided warfare with whites but resisted when the government took possession of Nez Perce land.** *Above:* **A descendant of the Nez Perce He-Yum-Ki Yum-Mi, who fought alongside Chief Joseph, joins in a summer parade, 1985.**

what was the Nez Percé War. By the time Howard arrived with more men and heavy artillery, Joseph had moved across the Clearwater River.

It was Chief Joseph's plan to move the tribe north of the Canadian border where the US Army would not follow them, but to do so they would have to reach Montana, and cross the Rockies and hundreds of miles of plains. They crossed into Montana near Fort Missoula and managed to either elude or defeat the Army in a series of actions that took them across the Continental Divide and through newly established Yellowstone National Park. As they struck out across the plains, they were pursued not only by Howard's troopers, but by the Seventh Cavalry under Colonel Nelson 'Bearcoat' Miles from Fort Keogh as well. The Nez Percé eluded the Seventh in a skirmish on Canyon Creek and crossed the Missouri at Cow Island on 23 September. A week later the exhausted Nez Percé, still moving their cattle and dependents along with the fighting force, camped in the Bear Paw Mountains. They were finally about a day's ride from Canada. Howard was still two days behind, and Joseph relaxed. Meanwhile, however, Miles managed to get a sizable cavalry force within striking distance. The force took a large number of casualties but managed to surround Joseph almost within sight of Canada. A battle raged for five days, with the Army bringing up Hotchkiss guns to pound the encampment that the cavalry had surrounded. Finally, with no hope left, Joseph was forced to surrender on 7 October 1877, when he delivered his most eloquent and remembered words:

Tell General Howard I know his heart. What he told me before I have in my heart. I am tired of fighting. Our chiefs are killed. Looking Glass is dead. Toohoolhoolzote is dead. The old men are all dead. It is the young men who say yes or no. He who led on the young men is dead. It is cold and we have no blankets. The little children are freezing to death. I want to have time to look for my children and see how many of them I can find. Maybe I shall find them among the dead. Hear me, my chiefs! I am tired; my heart is sick and sad. From where the sun now stands I will fight no more forever.

A few of the Nez Percé managed to get across the border and link up with Sitting Bull's Sioux, but the bulk of the survivors were sent, not back to Lapwai as promised by Miles, but to Indian Territory instead. In 1885 what was left of the tribe was returned to Lapwai, but Joseph was sent to the Colville Reservation in Washington State, where he died on 21 September 1904.

In 1950 the Nez Percé tribe had a population of 1400, which increased to 2251 by 1970. In 1985 the Nez Percé Reservation in Idaho had a population of 2015.

Niantic
Geographic Region: Northeast (south of Cape Cod)
Linguistic Group: Algonquian
Principal Dwelling Type: Rectangular barrel-roofed house
Principal Subsistence Type: Fish

Nipissing
Geographic Region: Northeast (northern Great Lakes country)
Linguistic Group: Algonquian

Below: **Mounted Nez Perce Indians in full ceremonial regalia. This photograph, taken in 1906, occurred long after Chief Joseph was forced to surrender Nez Perce land to the government.**

Principal Dwelling Type: Crude conical tipi

Principal Subsistence Type: Wild game

Nipmuck

Geographic Region: Northeast (central Massachusetts)

Linguistic Group: Algonquian

Principal Dwelling Type:
Rectangular barrel-roofed house

Principal Subsistence Type:
Hunting, fish, maize

The Nipmuck were a major tribe in central Massachusetts in the mid-seventeenth century. They were joined by King Philip (Metacomet) and the Wampanoag in 1674 after the latter were driven west by the English. They were a major power in the subsequent King Philip's War of 1675–76 in which they were allied with the Wampanoag and Narragansett under King Philip. The war ended with the resounding defeat of the three tribes by the English and the eventual extinction of the Nipmuck as a separate tribe.

Nisenan, Nishinam (*see* Maidu)

Nishga (*see* Tsimshian)

Nisqually (Nisquali)

Geographic Region: Northwest Coast (southern Puget Sound, Washington)

Linguistic Group: Salishan

Principal Dwelling Type:
Rectangular plank house

Principal Subsistence Type: Fish

In 1985 the population of the Nisqually Reservation in Washington stood at 1726.

Nitinat

Geographic Region: Northwest Coast (West Vancouver Island)

Linguistic Group: Algonquian-Wakashan

Principal Dwelling Type:
Rectangular plank house

Principal Subsistence Type: Fish

No Bows (*see* Sioux)

Nooksack (Nooksak)

Geographic Region: Northwest Coast (Puget Sound, Washington)

Linguistic Group: Salishan

Principal Dwelling Type:
Rectangular plank house

Principal Subsistence Type: Fish

In 1985 the population of the Nooksack Reservation in Washington stood at 860.

Nootka (Aht)

Geographic Region: Northwest Coast (Vancouver Island, British Columbia)

Linguistic Group: Wakashan

Principal Dwelling Type:
Rectangular plank house

Principal Subsistence Type: Fish, whaling

Linguistically and culturally related to the Heiltsuk and Kwakiutl, the Nootka (known locally as Aht) are also related to the Makah. The Nootka, like most tribes of the Northwest, were very accomplished fishermen and boat builders. They were

Above: **A group of Omaha boys in cadet uniforms, dressed for Pennsylvania's Carlisle Indian School in 1879.** *Opposite:* **Osage council member Joseph Matthews, seated in front of his fireplace at his home in Oklahoma, 1937. During the 1930s, self-government on reservations was promoted and education improved. Matthews himself was also an author, a historian, and a Rhodes scholar.**

among the few tribes of the region to engage in whaling. Characteristic of the Nootka are the *tamanwa,* sacred dramas based on tribal legend. Another tradition of the tribe, which is shared with other Northwest Coast tribes, is the potlatch ceremony *(see also* Haida and Kwakiutl).

Captain James Cook made contact with the Nootka in 1776 and, counting 95 canoes, estimated a population of 2000. In 1967 there were 3135 Nootka living in British Columbia.

Norridgewock

Geographic Region: Northeast (Maine)
Linguistic Group: Algonquian
Principal Dwelling Type: Crude conical tipi
Principal Subsistence Type: Wild game

The leading tribe of the Abnaki confederacy, the Norridgewock were first encountered by the white man on the Ken-

nebec River in Maine. In the long series of colonial wars between the French and English, they supported the French. A large number were converted to Catholicism by Jesuit missionary Sebastien Rasles, who arrived in 1689. In 1724 the English attacked the Norridgewock village, killing Father Rasles and 100 Indians. In 1754, at the start of the French and Indian War, the Norridgewock were again dispersed, after which they made their way to Canada, where their descendants still reside.

North Alaskan Eskimo (*see* Eskimo)

Northern Paiute (*see* Paiute)

Northern Wintun (*see* Wintun)

Nottaway
Geographic Region: Southeast (Virginia, North Carolina)
Linguistic Group: Algonquian
Principal Dwelling Type:
   Rectangular barrel-roofed house
Principal Subsistence Type: Maize

Nunamiut (North Alaskan Eskimo, *see* Eskimo)

Ocone (*see* Seminole)

Oglala Sioux (*see* Sioux)

Ohlone (*see* Costonoan)

Ojibwa (*see* Chippewa)

Okchai (*see* Creek)

Okinagan (Okanagan)
Geographic Region: Great Basin (southern British Columbia)
Linguistic Group: Salishan
Principal Dwelling Type:
   Semisubterranean house
Principal Subsistence Type: Large game
Subgroups: Lower Okinagan (Konkonelp, Conconcully)

In 1967 there were 1503 Okinagan.

Omaha

Geographic Region: Plains and Prairies
(Nebraska)
Linguistic Group: Siouan-Dhegiha
Principal Dwelling Type:
Prairie-Southwest earth lodge
Principal Subsistence Type:
Hunting, maize

Although they were related linguistically, the Omaha were never allied with the Sioux, and were frequently at war with them. The Omaha originally inhabited on both sides of the Mississippi River near present-day St Louis, from which they migrated at an early date to the lower Platte River and the Elkhorn Valley of Nebraska. In the treaties of 1830, 1836 and 1854 the Omaha ceded their lands to the US government. They were moved, along with the Winnebago, to a reservation in northeastern Nebraska, where they had an estimated population of 1600 in 1950 and 1300 in 1970.

Onandaga (*see* Iroquois)

Oneida (*see* Iroquois)

Osage (Wazhazhe)

Geographic Region: Plains and Prairies
(Kansas)
Linguistic Group: Siouan-Dhegiha
Principal Dwelling Type:
Prairie-Southwest earth lodge
Principal Subsistence Type:
Hunting, maize
Subgroups: Great Osage, Little Osage,
Arkansa Osage

Closely related to the Omaha, Kansa, Quapaw and Ponca, the Osage are thought to have once lived in the Ohio River valley, but they were first encountered by the white man in Missouri, where they were recorded as having large cornfields. They usually lived in earth lodges, but when on hunting trips to the northern plains in search of buffalo, they carried and used the plains tipi. During the first half of the eighteenth century, they were allied with the French against the Fox Indians. In 1804 they were encountered by Lewis and Clark, who estimated their population at 6500. Between 1808 and 1825 the Osage ceded most of their land to the US government in exchange for a reservation in Kansas, and on 15 July 1870 they were given a larger reservation in Indian Territory.

In 1904 oil drilling began on Osage land and in 1906 the wells produced over 5 million barrels. Oil production on their land helped to make the Osage one of the richest tribes in the United States by the mid-twentieth century.

The Osage population declined from 4102 in 1843 to 1582 in 1886, but increased to 2229 in 1906, the year that Oklahoma became a state. In 1985 the Osage Agency in Oklahoma had a population of 6743, up from 4972 in 1950.

Otchente Chakowin (*see* Sioux)

Oto (Otoe)

Geographic Region: Plains and Prairies
(Nebraska)
Linguistic Group: Siouan-Chiewere
Principal Dwelling Type:
Prairie-Southeast earth lodge
Principal Subsistence Type:
Hunting, maize

The Oto are linguistically related to the Missouri tribe and are usually considered to be one and the same. They are related to both the Iowa and Winnebago, and once lived in the Great Lakes region. When first contacted by the French about 1690, however, they were living on the Des Moines River in Iowa. They ceded their land to the US government in 1854, and settled on a reservation on the Big Blue River on the Kansas-Nebraska state line. They sold this land in 1881 and used the proceeds to buy land within Indian Territory. This in turn was divided among members of the tribe in 1907.

Like most tribes of the region, their numbers declined during the nineteenth century. From a population of 931 in 1843, they were reduced to 708 in 1862, 438 in 1880 and 377 in 1891. By 1907, when the Indian Territory land was divided, there were 514 members of the tribe among whom to divide it. In 1950 the population had increased to 930, and in 1985 the tribe numbered 1231.

Ottawa

Geographic Region: Northeast (northern
Great Lakes country)
Linguistic Group: Algonquian
Principal Dwelling Type: Domed bark,
thatch or hide house
Principal Subsistence Type: Fish, wild
game, wild rice

The name Ottawa is derived from the Algonquian *adawe,* meaning 'to trade,' an apt name for the tribe, who had an active trading relationship with the related Chippewa and Potawatomi as well as other tribes of the region. Like the Chippewa, they built birch bark canoes and harvested wild rice. They were visited by the French explorer Samuel de Champlain

Opposite: **Pontiac's Rebellion was called 'Pontiac's Conspiracy' by the whites because the Ottawa chief succeeded in uniting a confederation of 18 tribes against white settlement. His sessions of attacks lasted for three months.** *Above:* **Pontiac (c 1715-1769) was chief of the Ottawas and an influential leader. In 1766 he accepted a peace belt and attended the conference at Fort Ontario, but was murdered in Illinois by a Peoria Indian working under an English trader.**

in 1615, with whom they had friendly relations thereafter. The Ottawa were allied with the Huron, but after the destruction of that tribe by the Iroquois League, the Ottawa were pushed farther to the west into Michigan.

By 1755 Ottawa Chief Pontiac had risen to the forefront as one of the most important Indian leaders of the era. Widely respected by the other Algonquian tribes, Pontiac managed to form an alliance between the Ottawa, Chippewa, Potawatomi and his mother's people, the Miami. This alliance virtually dominated the entire Great Lakes region and served as sort of a western equivalent of the powerful Iroquois League. Friendly relations continued between Pontiac and the French. After the surrender of Montreal in September 1760 and the fall of New France, Pontiac met with the English commander, Major Robert Rogers, and told him that the English could occupy the former French forts if they treated the Indians with the same sort of respect they had received from the French. This was not forthcoming, and Pontiac led a general uprising that included not only the members of Pontiac's confederacy but neighboring tribes as well. The French encouraged these raids by implying their determination to recapture New France in Louisiana. In the spring of 1763, when he heard about the Treaty of Paris which, signed in February, had given vast tracts of Algonquian land to the English, Pontiac was enraged. He began a military campaign against the English that was of a persistence rarely seen in an undertaking by Indian tribes. Between 16 May and 21 June 1763, nine major forts or settlements, including Saulte Ste Marie, Mackinac and Green Bay, were plundered by Pontiac's Algonquian legions, and the existence of all the English settlements west of the Alleghenies was put in doubt. The turning point probably came with Pontiac's siege of Detroit, which lasted from May until it was abandoned without success at the end of July.

A major English counteroffensive came in 1765, which in turn resulted in the signing of a peace treaty the following year at Oswego. The Algonquian confederacy forged by Pontiac crumbled. Pontiac himself remained associated with the French until his assassination in 1769, at the age of 49, by an Illinois Indian in the employ of the English.

Between 1831 and 1836 the Ottawa were removed to Kansas from the Ohio area by the US government. In 1867 the Omnibus Treaty provided for the establishment of lands within Indian Territory for the last members of the Algonquian tribes.

In 1906 there were an estimated 4700 Ottawa in North America. In 1967 there were 1495 Ottawa in Canada, the nation whose national capital lies in their old sphere of influence and which is named for them. In 1985 there were 377 members of the Ottawa tribe living in Oklahoma.

Ousita (*see* Wichita)

Ozette

Geographic Region: Northwest Coast (northwestern Washington)
Linguistic Group: Salishan
Principal Dwelling Type:
    Rectangular plank house
Principal Subsistence Type: Fish

Pacaha (*see* Quapaw)

Pahvant (*see* Ute)

Paiute

Geographic Region: Great Basin (Utah, Nevada, eastern California)
Linguistic Group: Uto-Aztecan
Principal Dwelling Type: Crude conical tipi (wickiup)
Principal Subsistence Type: Wild plants, small game
Subgroups: Paiute Proper, Northern Paiute (Paviotso), Southern Paiute (Chemehuevi), Mono (eastern California)

Related to the Bannock, Shoshone, Gosiute and Ute, the Paiute were among the most wide ranging of the Great Basin tribes. Though centered in northern Nevada, the Northern branch reached the deserts of eastern Oregon and south toward California's Mojave Desert. The Southern branch spread from the Mojave in the west to the Colorado River country of south-central Utah.

Of all the tribes in North America those in the Great Basin had developed the least technologically and were the closest to our conception of the Stone Age lifestyle, except for the Paiute of Owens Valley, California, who practiced irrigation. Most of their food supply consisted of gathered roots and berries, and the hunting they did was with clubs rather than bows and arrows or spears. The jack rabbit was to the Paiute and other Basin peoples what the buffalo was to the Plains tribes, providing meat to eat as well as fur and leather for clothing and shelter. The Paiute hunted the jack rabbits frequently by driving them against nets and beating groups of them to death.

Because the Great Basin is such an arid and inhospitable country, the Paiute had little contact with the white man until the second half of the nineteenth century. With the discovery of major Comstock silver deposits in the Reno/Carson City area in 1859 and the completion of the transcontinental railroad in 1869, a large influx of settlers entered Paiute lands. Relations were good at first, but the white man and his grazing animals wreaked havoc on the sparse resources of the Basin.

Opposite: **Horse Chief, a Pawnee warrior painted by George Catlin. Despite their startling looks, the tribe was usually friendly toward whites and sent delegations to Washington.** *Above:* **Wovoka, or 'The Cutter,' was the son of Tavibo the prophet and was called the 'Messiah' of the Paiute tribe. He created the Ghost Dance religion, which promised an Indian messiah.**

The traditional Paiute lifestyle collapsed due to the culture shock of going directly from the Stone Age to the machine age. The Ghost Dance religion of the late 1880s originated with the Paiute shaman Wovoka in reaction to this disruption. It quickly spread to other Basin and Plains tribes, proclaiming that an Indian messiah would come and unite all Indian tribes against the whites. The Ghost Dance resulted eventually in a good deal of violence, especially among the Sioux, but the movement died out by the early 1890s when no messiah had yet appeared. Wovoka himself lived until 1932.

The majority of the Paiute still remain in Nevada, scattered across the state on small reservations. In 1985 there were 100 people at the Winnemucca Colony, 192 at the Lovelock Colony, 364 at the Yerington Colony, 643 at the Walker River Reservation, 678 at the Fort McDermitt Reservation, 721 at the Reno-Sparks Colony, and 1285 at the Pyramid Lake Reservation. In addition there were 345 members of the Paiute tribe of Utah and 2056 Paiute at four rancheria in California. There are also a small number of Paiute living on Shoshone ranches in those states.

Pakana (*see* Creek)

Palouse (Palus)
Geographic Region: Great Basin (eastern Washington)
Linguistic Group: Penutian-Sahaptin

Left: **Wolf Necklace, a Palouse chief. This tribe was well known for breeding Appaloosa horses, which were then traded with Indians from other regions.** *Opposite:* **A Pawnee earth lodge. These permanent structures were built of posts and beams covered with willow branches and mud, and were large enough to hold several families.**

Principal Dwelling Type:
  Semisubterranean house
Principal Subsistence Type: Large game, fish

Pamaunkey
Geographic Region: Northeast
Linguistic Group: Algonquian
Principal Dwelling Type:
  Rectangular barrel-roofed house
Principal Subsistence Type: Maize

Pana, Panana, Panamaha (*see* Pawnee)

Panamint (*see* Shoshone)

Pani, Panimaha (*see* Pawnee)

Panis (*see* Wichita)

Panka (*see* Ponka)

Papago
Geographic Region: Southwest
Linguistic Group: Uto-Aztecan
Principal Dwelling Type: Domed bark, thatch or hide house
Principal Subsistence Type: Wild plants, small game

Linguistically related to the Pima, the Papago originally lived south and southeast of the Gila River, around Tucson, Arizona and south into the Mexican state of Sonora. They are an agricultural people, who cultivate maize, beans, wheat and cotton, as well as raise livestock. They are also noted for their exquisite basketry.

In 1950 there were 6200 Papago, and in 1985 the Papago Agency in Arizona had a population of 22,501, including 7209 on the San Xavier Reservation and 895 on the Gila Bend Reservation.

Passamaquoddy
Geographic Region: Northeast (Maine, New Brunswick)
Linguistic Group: Algonquian
Principal Dwelling Type: Crude conical tipi
Principal Subsistence Type:
  Caribou, moose

The Passamaquoddy, along with the related Penobscot, were an early member of the Abnaki confederacy, a group of tribes allied with the French against the English. By the early eighteenth century, many

members of the tribe had converted to Catholicism, and many are still members of this faith.

In 1985 there were 550 Passamaquoddy at the Pleasant Point Reservation in Maine, and 520 at Indian Township, Maine.

Patwin

Geographic Region: Northern California (Colusa and Yolo counties)
Linguistic Group: Penutian
Principal Dwelling Type: Crude conical tipi
Principal Subsistence Type: Mix of animal and wild plant foods
Subgroups: Hill Patwin, River Patwin (Valley Patwin)

Traditionally associated with the Maidu and Wintun, the Patwin were among the later California Indians to have contact with the Spanish, in 1810. The tribe contracted smallpox from the Spanish during the 1837 smallpox epidemic, and lost many of its members. Alfred Kroeber, in his 1982 survey, estimated a peak population for the Patwin of 3800 in 19 villages, but other estimates run higher.

Paviotso (Northern Paiute, *see* Paiute)

Pawnee (Pani, Pana, Panana, Panamaha, Panimaha)

Geographic Region: Plains and Prairies (Nebraska)
Linguistic Group: Hokan-Caddoan
Principal Dwelling Type: Prairie-Southeast earth lodge
Principal Subsistence Type: Hunting, maize
Subgroups: Chaui (Grand), Kitkehahki (Republican), Pitahauerat Tappage) and Skidi/Skedee (Wolf). The Quiver-as noted by the explorer Coronado

were also probably Pawnee.

The Pawnee name may have derived from Caddoan *pariki,* meaning 'horn,' a reference to the peculiar manner in which the tribe wore the scalplock. The Pawnee lived in established villages similar to those of the Mandan. They practiced agriculture but also hunted buffalo on the plains part of the year. They had a complex religion unrelated to other Plains tribes that included offering female captives as a sacrifice to ensure abundant crops. This rite was abolished in an unpopular decree by the Skidi Chief Petalesharo.

The Pawnee were hostile to the Spanish but friendly to the French, who appeared in the late seventeenth century. After the 1803 purchase of Louisiana by the United States, the Pawnee had good relations with the United States, to whom they ceded most of their land. They accepted a reservation in Kansas in 1857 but, having done so, they suffered greatly from disease, grasshopper damage to their crops and raids from the hostile Sioux. Between 1872 and 1876 their population dropped from 2447 to 1521, and in 1876 they were moved to a new reservation in Indian Territory. Sixteen years later these lands were divided among the remaining 820 Pawnee or sold for white settlement. In 1985 the Pawnee in Oklahoma numbered 1997, up from 1149 in 1970.

Pend d'Oreille

Geographic Region: Great Basin (northern Idaho, northwestern Montana and British Columbia)
Linguistic Group: Salishan
Principal Dwelling Type: Semisubterranean house
Principal Subsistence Type: Large game, fish

One of the group of tribes dominated

by the Spokane, the Pend d'Oreille are related to the nearby Kalispel, Coeur d'Alene and the Flathead, with whom they share a reservation in Lake County, Montana.

Pennacook (Pennacock)

Geographic Region: Northeast (New Hampshire)
Linguistic Group: Algonquian
Principal Dwelling Type: Crude conical tipi
Principal Subsistence Type: Hunting, maize

The name Pennacook is Algonquian for 'a twisted place,' and was applied to a confederation of small Indian bands in the adjacent areas of New Hampshire, Maine and Massachusetts south of the Abnaki lands. During King Philip's War (1674-76) the Pennacooks were divided, with one group supporting Philip in his attacks against the whites, and the other group supporting their own chief, Passakonawa, who advocated neutrality. After the war, the Pennacook as a whole were pressured out of their traditional lands by the white settlers. After being dispersed into Canada, the descendants of the Pennacook were assimilated by other Algonquian tribes in Quebec.

Penobscot

Geographic Region: Northeast (Maine)
Linguistic Group: Algonquian
Principal Dwelling Type: Crude conical tipi
Principal Subsistence Type: Hunting, maize

The Penobscot, along with their neighbors the Passamaquoddy, were members of the Abnaki confederacy allied with the French (who had established a mission among the Penobscot in 1688) against the English. It was not until 1749 that a peace

Opposite top: **A Pomo basket. The Pomos are known for their skill at basketweaving, and use of feathers and shells to decorate special gift baskets.** *Opposite bottom:* **Laura Somersal, a Pomo-Wapo, instructs a Native American Studies class in the art of basketmaking.** *Above:* **Bill Benson holds up a feathered basket. The feathers gave the surface a velvet-like appearance.** *Below:* **The plainer baskets held food; decorated ones (at lower left) were given as gifts.**

Above left: **The Pequots violently resisted white colonization. The English retaliated and virtually eradicated the tribe.** *Above right:* **Pfc Ira Hayes, a Pima, preparing for a parachute jump at a training session. He was one of four US Marines who raised the American flag on Iwo Jima in 1945.**

treaty was signed with the English. After the American Revolution, the Penobscot were awarded a reservation near Bangor, Maine, where they still remain. In 1985 the Penobscot Reservation had a population of 1106.

Peoria, Peouaria (*see* Miami)

Pequot

Geographic Region:
  Northeast (Connecticut)
Linguistic Group: Algonquian
Principal Dwelling Type:
  Rectangular barrel-roofed house
Principal Subsistence Type:
  Hunting, maize

It is probable that the Pequot and Mohegan were originally part of the same tribe, with the latter breaking off from the Pequot tribe around 1634. The Pequot, who numbered about 3000 during the early seventeenth century, were particularly hostile to white settlement and conducted frequent, bloody raids. In May 1637 they were attacked by the English in their principal settlement along the Mystic River, thus precipitating the Pequot War. During the war, in which the English sought to completely destroy the tribe's war-making capability, the other tribes of the region remained neutral, and the En-

glish succeeded in forcing the main body of the tribe out of Connecticut. This group, under Chief Sassacus, attempted to obtain the support of the Mohawks. Instead, the Mohawks declared war on them, killing most of their number including Sassacus himself. The surviving Pequots were enslaved by both the Mohegans and the English, who sent them to the West Indies. After 1650 a few Pequots were allowed to resettle in Connecticut, but by 1850 the practically extinct tribe numbered only 40 persons.

Petun (*see* Tobacco)

Piankashaw (*see* Miami)

Picuris Pueblo (*see* Pueblo)

Piegan Blackfoot (*see* Blackfoot)

Pima

Geographic Region: Southwest
Linguistic Group: Uto-Aztecan
Principal Dwelling Type: Domed bark, thatch or hide house
Principal Subsistence Type: Wild plants, small game

Linguistically related to the Papago, the Pima traditionally lived throughout southern Arizona and in the Mexican state of Sonora. They are descended from the prehistoric Hohokam peoples, who built extensive agricultural irrigation systems in the region and are responsible for the adobe ceremonial center, Casa Grande. The Pima have no direct rela-

tionship with the prehistoric Hohokam, but their methods of making pottery and other aspects of their culture suggest a connection. In 1985 the Pima Agency in Arizona, which includes the Ak-Chin and Gila River reservations, had a total population of 11,106.

Pitahauerat (*see* Pawnee)

Pit River (*see* Achumawi, Atsugewi)

Piware (*see* Miami)

Pohogue (*see* Shoshone)

Point Hope (North Alaskan Eskimo, *see* Eskimo)

Pojoaque Pueblo (*see* Pueblo)

Pokanoket (*see* Wampanoag)

Polar Eskimo (*see* Eskimo)

Pomo

Geographic Region: Northern California (Russian River)
Linguistic Group:
  Hokan-Pomo (Kulanapan)
Principal Dwelling Type: Crude conical tipi
Principal Subsistence Type: Mix of animal and wild plant foods, especially acorns

The Pomo were a major tribe in the coastal hill country north of San Francisco Bay. Their customary range cen-

tered on the Russian River drainage and extended from the area around Clear Lake in the east to the Pacific Coast in the west. While the acorn was the key element of their subsistence, they also hunted in the hills and fished in Clear Lake in boats constructed from tule reed. In the eighteenth century there were roughly 8000 Pomo organized into 70 autonomous villages. Each village was headed by a chief and had a large, central semisubterranean dance hall or meeting house. Basket making was an art at which the Pomo excelled, and their baskets represented a high quality of beauty and workmanship. Pomo basket makers traditionally used willow, sedge root, bullrush root and redbud bark, which they wove into numerous designs by a combination of methods. Some baskets were decorated with woven-in designs of black or dull red that, though geometric in form, were the symbolic representations of many objects. The more highly decorated Pomo baskets were adorned with small feathers inserted in the stitches to give the outside of the basket a soft, velvet-like appearance. By the twentieth century the art form had largely died out, although a few skilled Pomo artisans remained. Notable among them was Laura Somersal, who taught at Sonoma State University into the 1980s.

The Pomo had very little contact with the Spanish or the Russians, who both had settlements in their area. It was not until after the 1849 Gold Rush that white men began settling in the Clear Lake/ Russian River area in large numbers. In

Above: **Garcia River men, photographed in 1906, dressed to play baseball.** *Below:* **A Pomo man, circa 1890, drilling holes in beads using the traditional method. Like other California tribes, the Pomos developed intricate handicrafts and artwork.**

1856 a Pomo reservation was established on the coast north of Bodega Bay, but in 1868 it was abolished and many of the Pomo returned to the Clear Lake area. In 1985 there were 688 Pomo on the rancheria at Dry Creek, Hopland, Manchester/ Point Arena, Middletown, Surphur Bank and Upper Lake (Clear Lake).

Ponca (Panka, Punka)
Geographic Region: Plains and Prairies (southern South Dakota)
Linguistic Group: Siouan-Dhegiha
Principal Dwelling Type:
   Prairie-Southeast earth lodge
Principal Subsistence Type:
   Hunting, maize

The Ponca, whose name denotes 'sacred head,' are closely related to the Omaha, Osage and Kansa who also speak the Siouan-Dhegiha dialect. When originally encountered by whites they were living in Nebraska, but because of raids by the Sioux, they agreed in 1877 to accept a reservation in Indian Territory near the Quapaw Agency. There were at that time 681 Ponca in Indian Territory (where they became known as 'hot country' Ponca); another 36 remained in Nebraska among the Omaha. In 1889 a new reservation was established in Nebraska and some of those in Indian Territory chose to move back.

In 1906, when Indian Territory became Oklahoma, the Ponca lands were divided among the 784 Ponca who remained there. In 1944 there were 916 Ponca in Oklahoma and 401 in Nebraska. By 1985 the Ponca tribe in Oklahoma numbered 2272.

Potawatomi
Geographic Region:
   Northeast (Wisconsin)
Linguistic Group: Algonquian
Principal Dwelling Type: Domed bark, thatch or hide house
Principal Subsistence Type:
   Hunting, maize
Subgroups:
   Citizen Potawatomi (Oklahoma), Prairie Potawatomi (Kansas), Forest Potawatomi (Wisconsin)

The Potawatomi were closely related to, and associated with, the Chippewa and the Ottawa. When first encountered by the white man, they were living near Green Bay, Wisconsin, but in the late seventeenth century they moved south of Lake Michigan onto lands once occupied by the Illinois. They were allied with the French and joined Ottawa Chief Pontiac in his 1763 offensive against the English. After the defeat of Pontiac and the French, the Potawatomi joined the English against the Americans. They participated the 1795 Battle of Fallen Timbers and in the War of 1812, losing to the United States in both instances. Most of the tribe, which numbered about 2500, were removed to Kansas in 1846, but a few returned to Wisconsin, where they were known as Forest Potawatomi. In 1868 many of those in Kansas were moved to and made citizens of Indian Territory. Thereafter they were known as Citizen Potawatomi, and those who stayed behind in Kansas were known as Prairie Potawatomi.

In 1908 there were 1768 Citizen Potawatomi in Oklahoma and 676 Prairie Potawatomi in Kansas. The respective 1985 populations were 1910 and 1326, and the Forest Potawatomi numbered 466.

Powhatan

Geographic Region: Northeast (Virginia and Maryland)
Linguistic Group: Algonquian
Principal Dwelling Type:
    Rectangular barrel-roofed house
Principal Subsistence Type: Maize

The Powhatan comprised a large confederation of Algonquian bands that first made contact with white men in 1607 when Captain John Smith arrived in the New World to establish his colony in Jamestown. Smith noted no fewer than 160 Powhatan villages and estimated their population at more than 8000. These villages were built around community meeting houses 25 to 100 feet in length, and on the outskirts the Powhatan raised corn and tobacco.

Foremost among the leaders in Powhatan history was Chief Wahusonacook (1550–1618), also known as Chief Powhatan, who was the tribal leader at the time of Captain Smith's arrival in Jamestown. In 1607 Smith was captured by Powhatan while on an expedition and would have been executed had it not been for the intercession of Wahusonacook's daughter, Pocahontas. Relations between Wahusonacook's Powhatans and the Jamestown settlers improved considerably when Pocahontas converted to Christianity and married one of the Englishmen, John Rolfe, in April 1613.

Mr and Mrs Rolfe returned to England

in 1616, where she died the following year. Wahusonacook died two years later and was replaced by his brother, Opechancano, who declared war on the English. Over the course of the next 14 years the Powhatan destroyed every English settlement in Virginia except Jamestown and killed 347 English settlers. Opechancano broke the peace treaty of 1636 in 1642 in a surprise attack that cost 500 English lives, but in the English counterattack the Powhatan were defeated and Opechancano was killed. By the mid-eighteenth century the Powhatan tribal identity had been almost completely destroyed by disease, intermarriage, and protracted warfare with whites and other tribes.

Prairie Potawatomi (*see* Potawatomi)

Pswanwapam

Geographic Region: Great Basin (central Washington)
Linguistic Group: Penutian-Sahaptin
Principal Dwelling Type:
    Semisubterranean house
Principal Subsistence Type: Fish

Above: **Pocahontas preventing Captain Smith's death. As an adult, she became a diplomat for her father, Chief Powhatan. When Smith left, Pocahontas went into retreat. She was taken by the whites in 1613 and converted to Christianity. She later married Englishman John Rolf, and after returning to England, she became ill and died in 1617.**

Pueblo

Geographic Region: Southwest (New Mexico)
Linguistic Group: Uto-Aztecan (Tanoan and Keresan)
Principal Dwelling Type: Rectangular adobe house (pueblo)
Principal Subsistence Type: Wild plants, maize, small game

The Pueblo name derives from the Spanish word for 'village'. A pueblo is a complex of adobe houses, frequently interconnected and occasionally multi-storied, much like a modern apartment complex. The Pueblo Indians are those who dwell in the pueblos, specifically the Tanoan- and Keresan-speaking peoples of the Rio Grande valley between present-day Santa Fe and Albuquerque, New Mexico and the desert west of Albuquerque.

Below: These present-day Laguna Pueblo buildings closely resemble the traditional structures that were built long before the whites reached the Southwest. The sundried mud brick 'apartments' housed many families, and were usually constructed in caves and on cliff sides. Mud was a plentiful material, and the Pueblos used it to make their dishes and cookware as well as their homes. The Christian church in the background is a modern development, since the Indians the Spanish met over 300 years ago strongly rebuffed attempts to convert them. *Right:* A man and woman of Laguna Pueblo, New Mexico wear traditional garments made of cloth in this nineteenth century photo. The woman's dress is always tied over the right shoulder. Both wear hard-soled buckskin moccasins. An example of the Laguna Pueblo pottery can be seen in the foreground.

The Hopi and Zuñi tribes are related to the Pueblo people and they originally lived in pueblos. However, these larger tribes are linguistically dissimilar and lived in villages over a wide area, whereas Pueblo villages were more self-contained units.

The pueblo, usually built against the face of a cliff, generally consists of connected houses that rise in receding terraces, with the roof of one being the door yard, or patio, of the next. Some pueblos are such that an entire community could be contained within a single interconnected complex. The Indians in the pueblos have been farmers for centuries, raising corn, beans, squash and tobacco on family plots within a five-mile radius of their homes. They hunted deer and rabbits for meat and used the skins to make clothing. Everything, right down to the seeds for the spring planting, was owned by the women, and descent was reckoned through the mother's side of the family. A Pueblo male would be a member of his mother's clan, making his sister's children part of his clan, but his own children part of his wife's clan. A man's role traditionally was to hunt and also to regulate the religious life of the tribe.

The first white man to stumble into the land of the Pueblos was Cabeza de Vaca, a Spanish sea captain marooned on the Texas coast who led his men on a 1000-mile trek across the Southwest in search of a Spanish outpost. After they finally reached civilization they told wild tales of seven cities of gold, which were probably nothing more than the late afternoon sun shimmering on the walls of a distant adobe pueblo. In 1540 Francisco Vasquez de Coronado led a mounted expedition up into the northern Rio Grand country, where, near the present city of Albuquerque, there was a concentration of Pueblos. Coronado pillaged the cities, finding no gold as expected, just corn and squash. The missionaries who went along to convert the savages not killed by the soldiers set up missions alongside new Spanish cities. In 1680, however, the Indians revolted and destroyed the Spanish post at Santa Fe. Twelve years later the Spanish came back, this time to stay.

Although much of Indian culture has been destroyed or lost throughout North America, it is prominent in the Southwest today. The pueblos are still thriving

Opposite: **Residents of the Santa Clara Pueblo, New Mexico, making pottery.** *Top right:* **A Jemez Pueblo elder and his daughter participate in the Inter-Tribal Indian Ceremonial at Gallup, New Mexico.** *Below right:* **Two Acoma Pueblo residents herd burros up the steep trail to their home.**

	1970 Population	1985 Population	Dialect
Rio Grande Pueblos			
(Northern Pueblos Agency)			
Nambe	237	391	Tanoan
Picuris	165	154	Tanoan
Pojoaque	60	83	Tanoan
San Ildefonso	319	612	Tanoan
San Juan	1255	1821	Tanoan
Santa Clara	916	2622	Tanoan
Taos	1470	1718	Tanoan
Tesuque	231	304	Tanoan
(Southern Pueblos Agency)			
Cochiti	700	970*	Keresan
Isleta	2356	3401	Tanoan
Jemez	1528	2177	Tanoan
Sandia	211	248	Tanoan
San Felipe	1340	2051*	Keresan
Santa Ana	422	531	Keresan
Santo Domingo	2058	3186	Keresan
Zia	479	616	Keresan
Western Pueblos**			
(Southern Pueblos Agency)			
Acoma	2512	3195	Keresan
(Laguna Agency)			
Laguna	4432	6764	Keresan
Related pueblo-dwelling tribes**			
Hopi**	6000	8952	Shoshonean
Zuñi	5352	7754	Zuñi

* 1982 data   **The larger Hopi and Zuñi tribes are linguistically dissimilar to the Pueblo peoples, but because they built pueblos they are sometimes listed among the Western Pueblos.

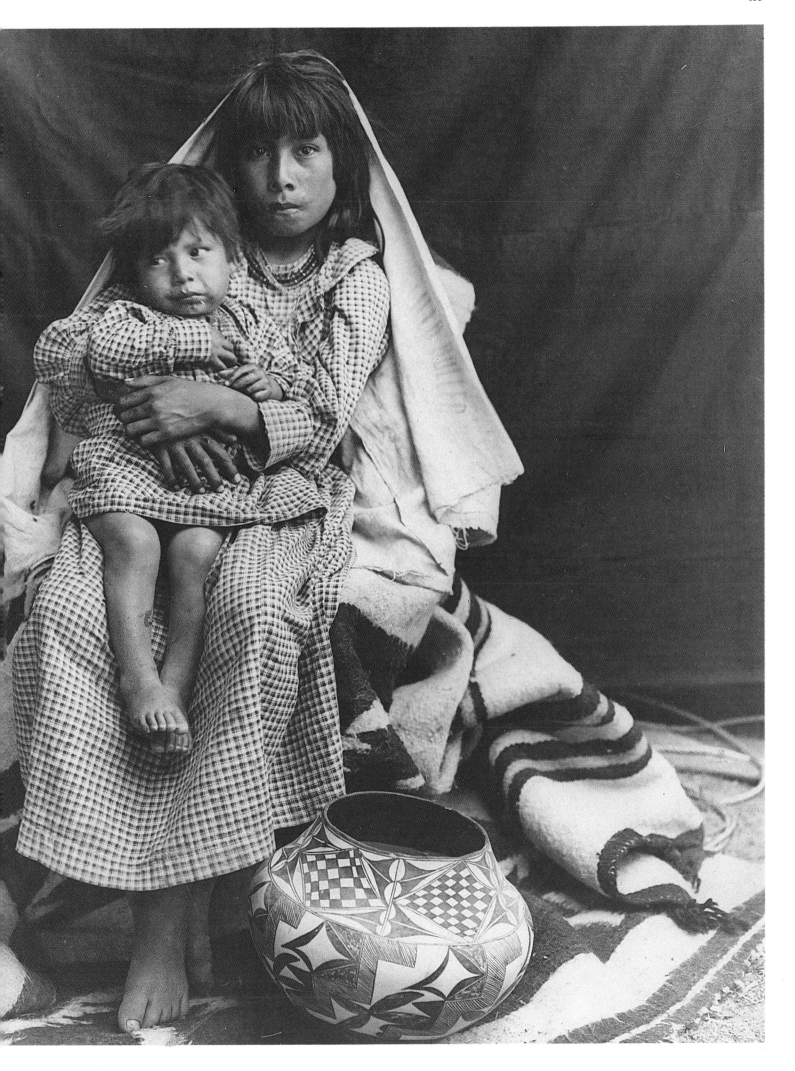

towns, the oldest continuously inhabited towns in North America. Pickup trucks and electricity are used, but otherwise life is surprisingly similar to what it must have been like centuries ago. The city of Taos, New Mexico near the Taos Pueblo, was reported by Citicorp Diners Club in 1984 to be one of the four largest art markets in dollar volume in the world, surpassed only by Paris, New York and neighboring Santa Fe. Much of the art being marketed features traditional Indian motifs and is executed by Indian artists.

Punka (*see* Ponca)

Puyallup
Geographic Region: Northwest Coast
    (southern Puget Sound, Washington)
Linguistic Group: Salishan
Principal Dwelling Type:
    Rectangular plank house
Principal Subsistence Type: Fish

The name Puyallup, which means 'generous people,' was also later adopted by the town near Tacoma, Washington, formerly known as Franklin. The Puyallup people still live on the nearby reservation, which had a population of 7158 in 1985.

Opposite: **Photographed in 1936 by Ansel Adams, Acoma Pueblo appears tranquil in the unrippled surface of a pool.** *Below:* **A resident of the Cochiti Pueblo in nothern New Mexico builds his house walls with adobe sun-dried bricks. Rooms are added wherever and whenever more space is needed. Not a nomadic tribe, the Pueblo tribes built their homes to last; some existing pueblos are almost 700 years old.** *Below bottom:* **A San Ildefonso Pueblo woman is baking bread. The adobe ovens resemble beehives.**

Opposite: Joe DeLaCruz, Quinault tribal chairman, speaks at Indian Daybreak Star Center in Seattle, Washington. The tribe won back its original lands under the protection of the conservation movement, and their beach is accessible only by special permit.

Above: Oliver Mason, hereditary chief of the Quinault Indian Nation and a direct descendent of Chief Taholah. *Below:* A Quinault tribal forestry crew plants new Douglas fir amid huge charred stumps on a burned-over site to prevent erosion.

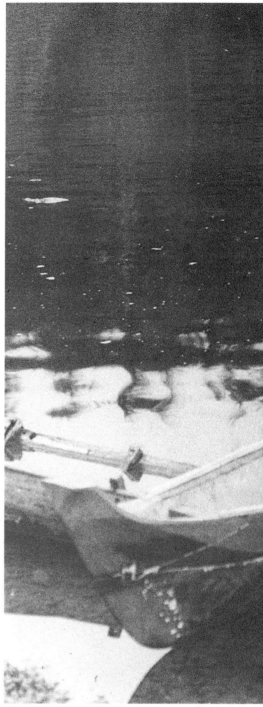

Quapaw (Pacaha, Capaha)
Geographic Region: Plains and Prairies
(northern Arkansas)
Linguistic Group: Siouan-Dhegiha
Principal Dwelling Type:
Domed thatched house
Principal Subsistence Type: Maize

The name Quapaw is derived from the term *Ugakhpa,* signifying 'downstream people.' It was applied to the tribe that was living on the Mississippi River near the mouth of the Arkansas River, and was first encountered by De Soto in 1541. The Quapaw are related to, and speak the same Siouan dialect as, the Osage, Omaha, Ponca and Kansa. In 1673 they cordially greeted the French explorers Jacques Marquette and Louis Joliet.

The Quapaw ceded most of their land to the US government in 1818, retaining a small reservation on the lower Arkansas River. In 1824 they sold the reservation and joined the Caddo. Later they moved to Indian Territory, where they lived among the Osage. By 1852 a Quapaw Reservation was surveyed in Indian Territory, but this reservation was overrun in the Civil War, and most Quapaw were still living among the Osage as late as 1878. Between 1887 and 1893 the Quapaw land was divided among members of the tribe, and the Quapaw Agency was established.

The first census of the Quapaw, conducted in 1784 by the Spanish, indicated that they numbered 708. In 1843 they numbered 476, and in 1885, after several decades of extreme hardship, their popu-

Above left: **Quinault Johnnie Saux, photographed in 1936, proudly displayed a chum, or dog, salmon.**
Above right: **Frank Tlyasman goes for a ride in his new dugout canoe in Quinault territory, Taholah, Washington.**

lation had declined to 174. In 1905 the population was 284, and the 1944 Indian Office census showed a population of 593. In 1985 the Quapaw tribe in Oklahoma numbered 1340.

Quechan
Geographic Region:
Southeastern California
Linguistic Group: Hokan-Yuman
Principal Dwelling Type: Domed bark, thatch or hide house
Principal Subsistence Type: Wild plants, small game

Queets (*see* Quinault)

Quileute

Geographic Region: Northwest Coast (western Washington)
Linguistic Group: Salishan
Principal Dwelling Type:
 Rectangular plank house
Principal Subsistence Type: Fish

In 1985 the Quileute Reservation had a population of 383, up from 270 in 1970. *(See also* Quinault)

Quinault

Geographic Region: Northwest Coast (western Washington)
Linguistic Group: Salishan
Principal Dwelling Type:
 Rectangular plank house

Principal Subsistence Type: Fish
Subgroups: Quileute, Queets

The Quinault are related to the Quileute, Chehalis and Chinook. The present-day Quinault Indian Nation is located on the Pacific Ocean coast of Washington's Olympic Peninsula, which is the original home of the tribe. As such, the Quinault are pleased to point out that they 'are among the small number of Americans who can walk the same beaches, paddle the same waters and hunt the same lands their ancestors did centuries ago.'

The Quinault traditionally lived in long-houses built of red cedar and fished for salmon and steel head trout in canoes, also made from cedar. These canoes included both small river canoes and huge ocean-going vessels. The latter were used

for fishing and were probably also used when these very social people attended the annual gathering of tribes on the Columbia River.

The Spanish first arrived in the land of the Quinault on 16 July 1775 near the present town of Moclips. In 1779, after the first bloody encounter, the Spanish established a mission. The US government created the Quinault Reservation on original Quinault land in keeping with the terms of a treaty signed in Olympia, Washington on 1 July 1855. Subsequent efforts to consolidate all of the Washington coastal tribes onto the Quinault Reservation after 1890 failed, however.

Beginning in 1922, large-scale commercial logging began on the Quinault Reservation. Because there was no forest

management plan in place at the time, much of the logged land was left open to erosion. The slash that piled up in the wake of the logging resulted in several serious forest fires over the next 20 years. After 1974 the tribal forestry program underwent a complete metamorphosis. With the help of private industry, government agencies and academic institutions, a comprehensive approach to fully develop the potential of Quinault forest resources was undertaken, and the Forestry Division within the Department of Natural Resources was established. While the forests constitute the Quinault Nation's greatest economic resource, steps have been taken to preserve other resources as well. In 1969 the reservation's 25 miles of ocean beach were closed to the public for conservation reasons and subsequently restored to a primitive state.

It is still possible for the general public to visit these areas and fish on Quinault Lake, but special permits and guides are required. For those without the time or inclination to fish the waters of the Quinault Reservation, Quinault Tribal Enterprises at Taholah, Washington, on the southern edge of the reservation, has brought out a line of seafood products under the *Quinault Pride* label. These include salmon, oysters and razor clams, all smoked over alderwood coals, the traditional method used by the coastal tribes to preserve such foods.

Above: Cooking salmon the Quinault way. *Right:* A tribal crew removes salmon eggs for hatching.

In 1985 there were 2013 people living on the Quinault Reservation, up from 1050 in 1970.

Quiveras (*see* Pawnee)

Quon-di-ats (*see* Ute)

R

River (*see* Mahican)

River Patwin (*see* Patwin)

River Wintun (*see* Wintun)

Rock Creek
Geographic Region: Great Basin (central Oregon along Columbia River)
Linguistic Group: Penutian-Sahaptin
Principal Dwelling Type: Crude conical tipi
Principal Subsistence Type: Mix of animal and wild plant foods

Sac (*see* Sauk)

Sahaptini (*see* Nez Percé)

St Lawrence Island Eskimo (*see* Eskimo)

Salina (Salinan)
Geographic Region: California (head-waters of the Salinas River)
Linguistic Group: Hokan
Principal Dwelling Type: Domed bark, thatch or hide house
Principal Subsistence Type: Acorns

Sallumiut (Baffin Island Eskimo, *see* Eskimo)

Salteaux (*see* Chippewa)

Samish
Geographic Region: Northwest Coast (Puget Sound, Washington)
Linguistic Group: Salishan
Principal Dwelling Type: Rectangular plank house
Principal Subsistence Type: Fish

Sandia Pueblo (*see* Pueblo)

San Felipe Pueblo (*see* Pueblo)

San Ildefonso Pueblo *(see* Pueblo)

San Juan Pueblo (*see* Pueblo)

San Nicoleño
Geographic Region: Southeastern California
Linguistic Group: Uto-Aztecan
Principal Dwelling Type: Domed bark, thatch or hide house
Principal Subsistence Type: Acorns, maize
The San Nicoleño were one of the 'mission peoples' tribes who became associated with the Spanish very early after the latter's arrival in California. According to Alfred Kroeber's 1925

Opposite: **An 1847 daguerreotype of the Sauk chief Kiyokaga ('One Who Moves About Alert'), or Watchful Fox. To avoid war, the Sauks ceded their territory in Michigan to the United States government and moved onto the plains. Their relocation released the last hold Indians had on Northeastern land.**

survey, the San Nicoleño, along with the Gabrieleño and Fernandeño, had an aboriginal population of about 5000.

Sanpoil
Geographic Region: Great Basin (southern British Columbia)
Linguistic Group: Salishan
Principal Dwelling Type: Semisubterranean house
Principal Subsistence Type: Fish, large game

Sans Arc (*see* Sioux)

Santa Ana Pueblo (*see* Pueblo)

Santa Clara Pueblo (*see* Pueblo)

Santee Sioux (*see* Sioux)

Santo Domingo Pueblo (*see* Pueblo)

Sanya (*see* Tlingit)

Sarsi
Geographic Region: Plains and Prairies (Upper Saskatchewan)
Linguistic Group: Athapascan (language isolate)
Principal Dwelling Type: Plains tipi
Principal Subsistence Type: Buffalo

Satsop
Geographic Region: Northwest Coast (Washington coast)
Linguistic Group: Salishan
Principal Dwelling Type: Rectangular plank house
Principal Subsistence Type: Fish

Satudene (*see* Bear Lake)

Sauk (Sac)
Geographic Region: Northeast (Wisconsin River)
Linguistic Group: Algonquian
Principal Dwelling Type: Domed bark, thatch or hide house
Principal Subsistence Type: Hunting, maize
The Sauk were originally to be found in eastern Michigan, but in the eighteenth century they migrated to Wisconsin, where they became united with the Fox. In the early part of the nineteenth century, the Fox migrated to Iowa without the Sauk. In 1832 a group of Sauk, under Chief Black Hawk, declared war on the whites. Black Hawk had fought under Tecumseh and had visions of himself at the head of a great confederacy of tribes like those of Tecumseh and Pontiac. As it turned out, Black Hawk was unable to get

the support of either the Fox or a large part of his own tribe, who remained at peace with the whites under the leadership of Chief Keokuk. Black Hawk's War was a series of running battles with US Army troops that ended when the chief was finally defeated on 3 August 1832. Black Hawk was taken into custody and President Andrew Jackson recognized Keokuk as he one chief of a unified Sauk and Fox, was relocated first to Iowa, then to Kansas.

In 1859 the political union of the two tribes was terminated and the Fox once again moved to Iowa. In 1867 the Sauk ceded their land in Kansas to the US government for land in Indian Territory. The two tribes were united for the last time in 1885 as the Sauk and Fox Nation under the leadership of Chief Ukquahoko.

The famous Columbia University anthropologist William Jones was a member of the tribe, as was Jim Thorpe, who won the pentathlon and decathlon at the 1912 Olympic Games in Stockholm.

In 1940 the Sauk and Fox population was 1512, with 473 in Iowa (mostly Fox), 129 in Kansas (mostly Sauk), and 910 in Oklahoma (mostly Sauk). In 1970, out of a total of 2041 there were 795 in Iowa, 250 in Kansas and 996 in Oklahoma. In 1985 the Sauk and Fox population stood at 1842, with 745 in Iowa, 56 in Kansas and 1041 in Oklahoma.

Sawokli (*see* Seminole)

Secotan
Geographic Region: Northeast
Linguistic Group: Iroquoian
Principal Dwelling Type: Rectangular barrel-roofed house
Principal Subsistence Type: Maize

Sekanai
Geographic Region: Subarctic (eastern mountains of interior British Columbia)
Linguistic Group: Athapascan
Principal Dwelling Type: Double lean-to, crude conical tipi
Principal Subsistence Type: Caribou, moose

Selawikmiut (North Alaskan Eskimo, *see* Eskimo)

Semiahmoo
Geographic Region: Northwest Coast (Northwestern Washington-British Columbia border)
Linguistic Group: Salishan
Principal Dwelling Type: Rectangular plank house
Principal Subsistence Type: Fish

Above: Although Catlin's painting portrays a warrior in full battle regalia, Chief Keokuk favored peaceful relations with whites. He dealt directly with the United States government, and was invited to Washington in 1833 and 1837. His rival, Black Hawk, sided with the British during the War of 1812 and fought the Americans in the Midwest. President Andrew Jackson recognized Keokuk as the chief of a united Sauk tribe, and then relocated him to Kansas.

Opposite: Osceola, a young Creek warrior, assumed leadership of the Seminole tribe in an attempt to prevent government possession of Indian land. Officials threw him in jail when he slashed the proposed treaty with his knife. Once freed, he disappeared with his forces into the swamps, where he conducted raids on settlers and earned the nickname 'Snake of the Everglades'. In 1837 he was tricked into a peace council, where he was seized and imprisoned.

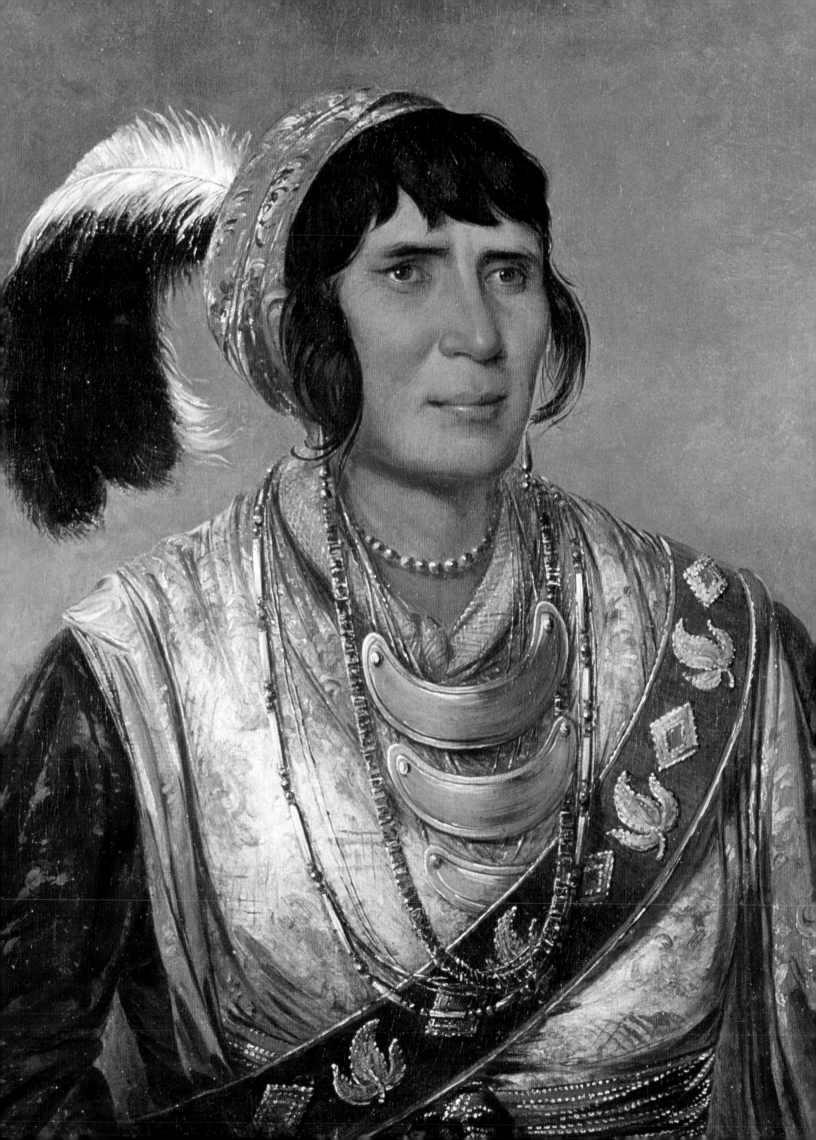

Above: **This 1941 photo shows two Seminole women cooking cane syrup.** *Opposite:* **Micanopy, a Seminole chief. The peace medal he wears conflicts with his warrior nature.**

Seminole

Geographic Region: Southeast (Florida)
Linguistic Group: Muskogean
Principal Dwelling Type:
　Rectangular thatched house
Principal Subsistence Type: Mix of wild
　and cultivated food sources
Subgroups: Alachua, Apalachee, Apachi-
　cola, Ays, Chiaha, Mayucas, Mikasuki
　(Miccosukee), Ocone (Oconee), Sawok-
　li, Tegesta, Timuqan, Tocabago

The Seminole were originally a branch of the Creek tribe, with whom they share a common language. Their name is derived from the Creek word for 'runaway.' The nucleus of the Seminole was the Ocone band, who lived on the Oconee River in Georgia as late as the early seventeenth century. By the end of that century, the Seminole, then considered separate from the Creek, had migrated south and became the dominant Indian tribe in Florida. The tribe grew even larger when it absorbed the influx of runaway slaves and the Creeks who came south as refugees of the 1813–14 Creek War.

By that time, white settlers in Georgia were beginning to complain that Spain's ineffective government in Florida was doing nothing to halt cross-border raids by the Seminole. US Army actions against the raiders in 1816 led to the First Seminole War, which ended with General Andrew Jackson's unauthorized invasion of Florida and his capture of Pensacola. Jackson succeeded in putting a temporary halt to the Seminole raids and the United States then bought Florida from the Spanish.

The guerrilla warfare continued through the 1820s, but by 1832 the situation seemed resolved. By the treaties of Payne's Landing (1832) and Fort Gibson (1834), the Seminole agreed to move west of the Mississippi if new lands could be found. In November 1835, however, Chief Osceola (1804–38) began the Second Seminole War by killing a rival chief who favored removal and by ambushing and massacring a US Army detachment under Major F L Dade. The US Army sent a 10,000-man force into the Florida jungle in search of the 4000-man army of Osceola, who soon earned the nickname

Opposite: **A Seminole woman grates kunti (samia) roots.** *Above:* **Billy Bowlegs, leader of the tribe during the third Seminole War.**

'Snake of the Everglades.' By March 1837, after over a year of fighting, the Seminole were largely defeated. Osceola himself was captured in October and put in irons at Fort Moultrie, where he died in 1838. A peace treaty was concluded in 1839 with provisions permitting the Seminole to remain in Florida rather than be removed to the west. The Indians promptly broke the treaty, and when the Second Seminole War finally ended in 1842, 3930 Seminole out of a total population of 4230 were removed to Indian Territory. The Seminole that remained in Florida eluded capture until the government lost interest. When a treaty was finally signed in 1934, it was publicized as ending the longest war in history.

In 1845 the Seminole in Indian Territory were placed under Creek administration, which they reluctantly accepted until they were assigned a tract of land of their own in 1856. In 1866, after having been allied with the Confederate States of America in the Civil War, the Seminole sold their land and bought a new tract of land, which served as the Seminole Nation until Oklahoma statehood in 1906.

At the time of the first US government census of the Seminole in Florida in 1823, the tribe had a population of 4883. At the time of Oklahoma statehood there were 2138 Seminole in Oklahoma. In 1950 there were 1070 Seminole in Oklahoma and 800 in Florida. In 1985 there were 3869 Seminole at the Wewoka Agency in Oklahoma and 1376 at the Seminole Agency in Florida.

Seneca (*see* Iroquois)

Serraño
Geographic Region: Southeast California
Linguistic Group: Uto-Aztecan
Principal Dwelling Type: Domed bark, thatch or hide house
Principal Subsistence Type: Mix of animal and wild plant foods

The Serraño were one of the 'mission peoples' tribes who embraced Spanish culture and religion soon after the arrival of the Spaniards. In 1882 there were 381 Serraño living in California. In 1985 there were 965 people at Morongo Reservation, 89 at San Manuel Reservation and 11 at Twenty-nine Palms Reservation.

Shasta
Geographic Region: Northwest California
Linguistic Group: Hokan-Shasta
Principal Dwelling Type: Semisubterranean house
Principal Subsistence Type: Mix of animal and wild plant foods

Shawnee
Geographic Region: Southeast (Cumberland Basin of the Tennessee River)
Linguistic Group: Algonquian
Principal Dwelling Type: Domed bark, thatch or hide house
Subgroups: Eastern Shawnee, Absentee Shawnee

The Shawnee were the southernmost of the major Algonquian-speaking peoples, and their name is derived from Algonquian word for 'southerners.' They came into conflict with the Cherokee and Catawba during the early eighteenth century and were forced north from the Tennessee River Valley into the Ohio River Valley, where they became allied with the related Delaware. Originally, the Shawnee, like many other tribes of the region, had been allied with the French against the English. However, after the defeat of the French in 1763 in the French and Indian War, the Shawnee became friendly with the English and aided them during the American Revolution.

After the Revolution, the Shawnee emerged as a major force in opposing westward expansion by the white settlers. The frontier warfare led to their defeat by the US Army under General 'Mad Anthony' Wayne at the Battle of Fallen Timbers in 1795. In the subsequent Treaty of Greenville they ceded much of their land to the United States. In the early nineteenth century, a pair of Shawnee twin brothers rose to leadership within the tribe and fervently took up the cause against the US government. One of them,

Tenskwatawa (The Prophet), was a shaman and spiritual leader and the other, Tecumseh, became a chief and probably the most important leader in Shawnee history.

The brothers were 40 years old in 1808 when they established a city at the confluence of the Wabash and Tippecanoe rivers. On 7 November 1811, Indiana Territorial Governor (and later US President) William Henry Harrison attacked the Tippecanoe village while Tecumseh was away, defeating Tenskwatawa and destroying the brothers' hopes for a restoration of Shawnee dignity after the 1795 Greenville Treaty. Tecumseh returned to find his village and his dreams dashed to rubble, and he went to war against the United States. When the War of 1812 began, the Shawnee allied themselves with the English and Tecumseh himself was commissioned as a brigadier general in the British Army. He was killed in the Battle of the Thames in 1813, but his brother, The Prophet, lived on. His mystical teachings are said to have

played a part in stirring up the trouble that led to the Creek War of 1813–14. Tenskwatawa went to Canada under British protection and did not return until 1826.

Tenskwatawa died in 1837. Three years later, William Henry Harrison and his running mate, John Tyler, were elected president and vice-president campaigning under the slogan 'Tippecanoe and Tyler too.' When Harrison died within a few weeks of his inauguration, there was some talk of Tenskwatawa placed a curse of death placed on him.

In 1831 the Shawnee sold their lands and joined other Shawnee who had been living in Kansas. Between 1845 and 1867 they moved again, this time to Indian Territory. The first Shawnee to arrive in Indian Territory became known as East-

Left: **Tecumseh, chief of the Shawnees, was a well respected leader and a humane warrior. He often sought the advice of his twin brother Tenskwatawa, also known as The Prophet,** *right.* *Below:* **The camp of Shoshone chief Washakie, 1870.**

ern Shawnee, and the later arrivals were known as Absentee Shawnee. They were officially organized into tribes in 1939.

In 1909 there was a total of 1388 Shawnee in Oklahoma. In 1944 there were 308 Eastern Shawnee at the Quapaw Agency in Oklahoma and 731 Absentee Shawnee at the Shawnee Agency in Oklahoma. In 1985 the Eastern Shawnee tribe had a population of 377.

Sherry-dika (*see* Shoshone)

Shinnecock
Geographic Region: Northeast (Long Island, New York)
Linguistic Group: Algonquian
Principal Dwelling Type: Dome-shaped thatch house
Principal Subsistence Type: Hunting, maize, fish

The descendants of the Shinnecock still numbered 160 as late as 1950, but by that time they had abandoned their original language and culture.

Shoshone (Shoshoni)
Geographic Region: Great Basin (Colorado, Idaho, Nevada, Utah and Wyoming)
Linguistic Group: Uto-Aztecan
Principal Dwelling Type: Crude conical tipi
Principal Subsistence Type: Mix of animal and wild plant foods
Subgroups: Boise, Box Elder, Bruneau, Digger, Green River Snake (Snake, Kogohue), Koso (Panamint), Lemhi (Agaiduka), Pohogue, Sherry-dika, Tosawi, Tukadka, Wind River

The Shoshone were the most wide-ranging of the Great Basin tribes, with a habitat that stretched from the eastern Oregon desert to southern Colorado. They were closely related to the Bannock, Gosiute, Paiute and Ute, with whom they shared these lands and with whom there was a good deal of intermarriage.

Of all the tribes in North America, those in the Great Basin were the least developed technologically and the closest

Opposite: **Steep Wind, a Sioux chief, in full military dress. Each feather was a reward for a deed in battle. The red detail and beaded crown are typical Sioux decorations as seen in the 1890 warbonnet,** *right.*

to our conception of the Stone Age lifestyle. Most of their food supply consisted of gathered roots and berries. Hunting was done with clubs rather than bows and arrows or spears, and usually involved small game such as jack rabbits.

Because the Great Basin is such an arid and inhospitable country, the Shoshone, like the Paiute and other related tribes, had little contact with the white man until the nineteenth century. Today, many of them still live on reservations scattered throughout their old lands.

Among the most famous of the Shoshone people was a woman named Sacagewea (Bird Woman). At about age 12 she was captured by a Crow raiding party and sold to the Mandan across the Rockies on the upper Missouri River. In 1804, when Sacagewea was 18, Lewis and Clark passed through Mandan country enroute to the Pacific. They met her and asked her to guide them across the Rockies. She proved extremely valuable as a guide and interpreter, and was especially helpful in obtaining supplies from the tribes they encountered on their travels. She accompanied the explorers all the way to the Pacific and was reunited with the Shoshone on the return trip in 1806.

In 1985 there were 140 people at Duckwater Reservation, Nevada; 494 at Elko Colony, Nevada; 134 at South Fork Colony, Nevada; 154 at Yomba Reservation, Nevada, and 314 at Battle Mountain Colony, Nevada, along with a number of Shoshone sharing reservations with other tribes, such as the Paiute in Nevada, California and Idaho.

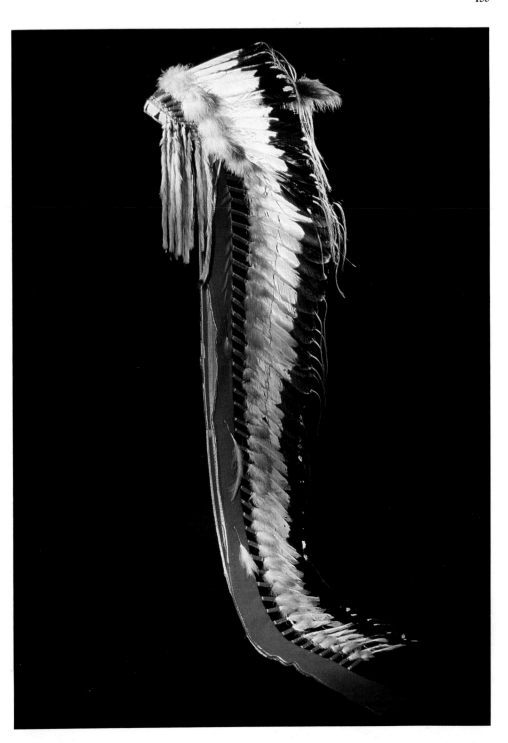

Shushwap
Geographic Region: Great Basin (Fraser River valley, British Columbia)
Linguistic Group: Salishan
Principal Dwelling Type:
   Semisubterranean house
Principal Subsistence Type: Large game, fish
   In 1967 the Shushwap in Canada numbered 3675, up from 220 in 1950.

Siksika (*see* Blackfoot)

Sinkaietk
Geographic Region: Northwest Coast (north-central Washington)
Linguistic Group: Salishan
Principal Dwelling Type:
   Rectangular plank house
Principal Subsistence Type: Fish

Sinkquaius
Geographic Region: Great Basin (eastern Washington)
Linguistic Group: Sahaptin
Principal Dwelling Type:
   Semisubterranean house
Principal Subsistence Type: Fish, game

Sioux (Dakota, Lakota, Nakota, Otchente Chakowin)
Geographic Region: Plains and Prairies
Linguistic Group: Siouan (Dakotan)
Principal Dwelling Type: Plains tipi
Principal Subsistence Type: Buffalo
Subgroups: Eastern or Santee group—M'dewakanton, Santee, Sisseton, Wahpekute, Wahpeton
   Central group—Yankton, Yanktonai (Little Yankton)

Western or Teton group—Blackfoot Sioux (unrelated to the Blackfoot tribe), Brulé, Hunkpapa, Miuneconjou, Oglala, Sans Arc (No Bows), Teton, Two Kettle. (The members of the Teton group other than the Brulé and Oglala were known as the same group in ancient times.)
Note: The Siouan-Dhegiha-speaking peoples of the southern plains such as the Kansa, Iowa, Omaha, Osage, Ponca and Quapaw were occasionally referred to as the 'Southern Sioux' only because of the linguistic similarities. These tribes were independent tribes and had only an occasional passing association with the three major Dakota groups listed above.

The Sioux were the masters of the North American Plains and Prairies, feared by other tribes from the Great Lakes to the Rockies. With an aboriginal population of more than 30,000, they were one of the largest tribes in the Western Hemisphere. The name Sioux derives from the Chippewa word *nadowessioux,* meaning 'snake' or 'enemy.' The tribe called itself Dakota in the Santee dialect, Lakota in the Teton dialect or Nakota in the Yankton dialect. The respective language dialects were referred to by the same terms, which in Siouan mean 'allies.' The tribe also referred to itself as Otchente Chakowin, or 'Seven Council Fires,' also a reference to the major allied subgroups of the tribe.

The Sioux migrated to the upper Plains states from the headwaters of the Mississippi in the sixteenth century because of warfare with the Cree. After the move west, a long-standing feud with the Chippewa continued on their flank, while they found themselves coming into conflict with the Arikara, Cow and Pawnee on the plains. By the nineteenth century the Sioux had mastered the strife by acquiring horses and guns, and had formed an alliance with the Cheyenne and Arapaho.

Because of the conflict with the Chippewa, those Sioux living in the east were willing to cede their lands to the US government in 1830, and those in Minnesota followed suit between 1849 and 1851. The Sioux had relatively little contact with the white man prior to the middle of the nineteenth century, but the situation changed for the worse after 1862. The Sioux Wars, which lasted for essentially 38 years, were the bloodiest of all the Indian wars that were fought in North America.

In 1862 Chief Little Crow and the M'dekakantons massacred 644 Minnesotans and attacked New Ulm and Fort Ridgely. Colonel Henry Sibley was finally able to defeat them at Wood Lake and to rescue 269 captives. In the west, the war-

fare against the whites had been sporadic. A wagon train had been attacked as early as 1841, and in 1854 a group of soldiers had been massacred near Fort Laramie. The Minnesota Sioux War, however, brought a general Sioux uprising. An expedition was mounted against the uprising in 1865. A treaty was proposed at Fort Laramie but rejected by Oglala Sioux Chief Red Cloud (Mahpiua-luta), who then escalated the war against the United States.

What came to be known as Red Cloud's War began in 1866. Colonel Henry Carrington had been detailed to establish a series of forts in Wyoming and Montana to protect the Bozeman Trail, when he was attacked on 21 December by Red Cloud's forces. Captain William Getterman's rescue column was intercepted and massacred to the last man. Red Cloud then besieged Fort Laramie itself. On 2 August 1867 another supply train, under Captain James Powell, was intercepted by the Sioux. This time the soldiers were equipped with rapid-fire rifles and were able to use the iron-reinforced wagon boxes as barricades. Powell's men held off repeated attacks, killing roughly 60 of their attackers, turning the 'Wagon Box Fight' into a defensive victory for the Army.

On 6 November 1868 Red Cloud signed a treaty at Fort Laramie by which he agreed to a cease-fire on the condition that the two new forts between Laramie and Bozeman be abandoned. Having won his war, Red Cloud was willing to accept a huge reservation that was set aside for the Sioux in Dakota territory. The reservation was, at that time, larger than the state of Pennsylvania and larger than any of the nations established in Indian Territory. From his headquarters at the Red Cloud (later Pine Ridge) Agency, the chief became a recognized and respected Sioux leader, and made several trips to Washington, DC on behalf of his people before

his death in 1909 at the age of 87.

The conclusion of Red Cloud's War brought a lessening of hostilities but by no means an end to them. Many of the Sioux continued the guerrilla war against the white settlers and the white soldiers. The major Sioux forces were led by Oglala Chief Crazy Horse and the Hunkpapa Chiefs Gall and Sitting Bull (actually Sitting Buffalo Bull, or Tatankya Iyotake), all of whom had participated in the fight during Red Cloud's War. Ignoring the Fort Laramie Treaty and the move to the Dakota Reservation, these groups continued to live in their old hunting grounds in the Yellowstone River drainage of southeastern Montana.

In 1876 US Army Chief of Staff, General William Tecumseh Sherman, asked his old Civil War colleague, Lt General Phil Sheridan, to organize a major summer offensive against the Sioux in Montana. The plan involved a three-pronged pincer, with General George Crook marching north from Fort Laramie, General John Gibbon east from Helena and General Alfred Terry west from Fort Abraham Lincoln (Bismarck). The heart of Terry's force was the Seventh Cavalry under Colonel George Armstrong Custer, the flamboyant cavalry leader who had so dramatically defeated the Cheyenne at the Battle of the Washita in 1868.

On 21 June 1876 Gibbon linked up with Terry, and Custer and the officers then met aboard the steamboat *Far West* on the Yellowstone River near Rosebud Creek to discuss strategy. Unknown to them, however, Crook had been defeated by Crazy Horse on the upper Rosebud on 17 June without having reached Montana, and he had withdrawn southward to regroup. In the absence of any word from Crook, Terry decided that they should move quickly to locate and engage the main body of Indians, which was thought to be somewhere in the upper Bighorn

River drainage, perhaps near the confluence with its tributary, the Little Bighorn. Custer's Seventh Cavalry was assigned to move south to search the Rosebud Creek drainage. Terry and Gibbon, with their slower infantry, progressed south on the Bighorn to meet Custer, who was to turn north on the Bighorn when he reached the headwaters of Rosebud Creek.

On 24 June, however, Custer detected signs of a large, recent Indian encampment. Fearing they might escape, he turned northwestward into the valley of the Little Bighorn to follow their trail. On the morning of 25 June, Custer's scouts sighted the Indians. They didn't realize that it was not just an Indian camp but perhaps the largest annual council in the history of the Plains tribes. There were eight branches of the Sioux tribe present, as well as members of the Northern Cheyenne as a guest tribe. There were more than 3000 people present at the council, and among them were hundreds of warriors, many of them fresh from the successful defeat of General Crook's column.

Leaving Captain Frederick Benteen and some of his cavalrymen to guard the pack train, Custer organized two attack columns. One, under Major Marcus Reno, would attack through the Little Bighorn Valley from the south, while Custer himself would lead the bulk of the Seventh Cavalry along the eastern ridge and attack the center of the encampment from above.

At 3 pm on 25 June, Reno met stiff resistance and was forced to withdraw. In the meantime, Custer had been detected. By 4 pm his troopers were under attack on the hillside above the Little Bighorn. Custer and his force of 215 men established a defensive position and attempted to fight off the attack, but they were no match for the overwhelming number of warriors led by Gall and Crazy Horse. Within 45 minutes, all 215 were dead.

The Sioux and Cheyenne broke camp and moved on before Terry and Gibbon arrived at the scene of the debacle. When news of the 'Custer Massacre' reached the national media, the public outcry forced the US Army to redouble its efforts to punish the Sioux and place the entire tribe on the reservation. General Nelson Miles

Above: Some famous Sioux warriors (left to right): Chief Red Cloud (Oglala), Chief Spotted Tail (Brule), brave Short Bull, brave Rain in the Face (Hunkpapa), Chief Gall (Hunkpapa), Chief Crow King, Chief Big Foot (Miuneconou), Chief Little Crow (Santee). Sitting Bull (*below*) was a Hunkpapa medicine man who became chief of his tribe. He led the Sioux in their victory against Custer.

located, defeated and captured Crazy Horse at Wolf Mountain on 7 January 1877 and chased Sitting Bull's band across the border into Canada, where they remained until 1881.

Crazy Horse was killed later in 1877 enroute to prison at Fort Robinson, Nebraska. Sitting Bull returned to the Sioux Reservation in 1881 and remained there until his death in 1890, except during his 1886 tour with Buffalo Bill's Wild West Show.

In 1890 the popularity of the Ghost Dance religion swept the Indian tribes of the Basin and Plains. This religion, to which a large number of Sioux at the reservation subscribed, taught that an Indian messiah would come among the tribes to unite all Indians, living and dead. The Ghost Dance itself was a bizarre ritual that stirred the Indians into a frenzy. This, in turn, frightened the whites living near the reservation. The Army, considering it to be the portent of another major uprising, went on alert and Sitting Bull was ordered to be arrested. When he was accidentally killed during the arrest on 15 December 1890, tensions increased dramatically. A band of Sioux, under the sickly Oglala Chief Big Foot,

Opposite: **The Santee Sioux Black Dog in 1835. His band attacked settlers in the 1862 Minnesota Uprising.** *Above:* **A detail from Red Horse's 1881 pictograph showing the Battle of Little Bighorn.** *Below:* **A Sioux cradleboard. The infant was placed inside and the device was strapped to the mother's back.**

fled to the badlands. They later surrendered to the Seventh Cavalry on 28 December. The following day, when the Army ordered the Indians disarmed, a shot was fired which touched off a firefight that ended with the death of 29 soldiers and 200 Indians, including women and children. This controversial massacre at Wounded Knee was the last battle of the Sioux wars. The next major shooting confrontation between the Sioux and the US government coincidently also took place at Wounded Knee, 83 years later, during the winter of 1973.

In 1970 there were 51,645 Sioux in the United States (including 37,380 in South Dakota alone), and another 2503 in Canada. This represented an increase over their total estimated 1950 population of 35,000.

In 1985 there were 18,754 Oglala Sioux at the Pine Ridge Reservation, 11,685 Teton Sioux at the Rosebud Reservation, 8443 Teton Sioux at the Standing Rock Reservation, 5150 Teton Sioux at the Cheyenne River Agency, 1082 Teton Sioux at the Lower Brulé Reservation, 4043 Sisseton Sioux at the Sisseton Reservation, 2355 Yankton Sioux at the Crow Creek Reservation, and 2929 Yankton

Sioux at the Yankton Reservation, for a total of 54,441 Sioux associated with South Dakota reservations. There were also 3162 Sioux in North Dakota, 422 Sioux in Nebraska, 5073 Sioux in Montana and 639 Sioux in Minnesota.

Sishiatl (*see* Sliammon)

Sisseton Sioux (*see* Sioux)

Sitka (*see* Tlingit)

Siuslaw
Geographic Region: Northwest Coast (central Oregon coast)
Linguistic Group: Penutian-Siuslaw
Principal Dwelling Type:
    Rectangular plank house
Principal Subsistence Type: Fish

Skagit
Geographic Region: Northwest Coast (southern Puget Sound, Washington)
Linguistic Group: Salishan
Principal Dwelling Type:
    Rectangular plank house
Principal Subsistence Type: Fish
    In 1970 the Skagit population stood at 259.

Skedee, Skidi (*see* Pawnee)

Skokomish
Geographic Region: Northwest Coast (Puget Sound, Washington)
Linguistic Group: Salishan
Principal Dwelling Type:
    Rectangular plank house
Principal Subsistence Type: Fish
    In 1970 the Skokomish population stood at 230, and in 1985 the Skokomish Reservation contained 1029 people.

Skykomish
Geographic Region: Northwest Coast (central Washington)
Linguistic Group: Salishan
Principal Dwelling Type:
    Rectangular plank house
Principal Subsistence Type: Fish

Slave
Geographic Region: Subarctic (Great Slave Lake, MacKenzie Territory)
Linguistic Group: Athapascan
Principal Dwelling Type: Double lean-to
Principal Subsistence Type:
    Caribou, moose, fish
    Named for the lake near which they live, the Slave numbered 3004 in 1967, making them the third largest of the Subarctic tribes after the Chipewyan and Carrier.

Above: **Modern examples of Sioux beadwork still show traditional tribal designs, shapes and styles. Medallions like these and other pieces were often for sale to the public.**

Sliammon (Sishiatl)
Geographic Region: Northwest Coast (southwest mainland British Columbia)
Linguistic Group: Salishan
Principal Dwelling Type:
    Rectangular plank house
Principal Subsistence Type: Fish

Snake, Green River (*see* Shoshone)

Snohomish
Geographic Region: Northwest Coast (Puget Sound, Washington)
Linguistic Group: Salishan
Principal Dwelling Type:
    Rectangular plank house
Principal Subsistence Type: Fish

Snoqualmi
Geographic Region: Northwest Coast (southern Puget Sound, Washington)
Linguistic Group: Salishan
Principal Dwelling Type:
    Rectangular plank house
Principal Subsistence Type: Fish

Sokoki (*see* Abnaki)

Songish
Geographic Region: Northwest Coast (United States side of the Straits Juan de Fuca)
Linguistic Group: Salishan

Principal Dwelling Type:
    Rectangular plank house
Principal Subsistence Type: Fish

South Alaskan Eskimo (*see* Eskimo)

Southampton Eskimo (*see* Eskimo)

Southern Paiute (*see* Paiute)

Spokane (Spokan)
Geographic Region: Great Basin (eastern Washington)
Linguistic Group: Salishan
Principal Dwelling Type:
    Semisubterranean house
Principal Subsistence Type: Fish, large game
    The Spokane were originally associated with the area around the present-day eastern Washington city that bears their name. They were the dominant tribe in a confederacy that included such tribes as the Kalispel, Coeur d'Alene and Pend d'Oreille. In 1970 there were 1500 Spokane, and in 1985 the Spokane Reservation had a population of 1961.

Squamish
Geographic Region: Northwest Coast (Hood Canal, Washington)
Linguistic Group: Salishan
Principal Dwelling Type:
    Rectangular plank house
Principal Subsistence Type: Fish

Staitan (*see* Kite)

Stikine (*see* Tlingit)

Stillaguamish
Geographic Region: Northwest Coast (Puget Sound, Washington)
Linguistic Group: Salishan
Principal Dwelling Type:
    Rectangular plank house
Principal Subsistence Type: Fish
    In 1985 the Stillaguamish tribe in Washington had a population of 482.

Stockbridge (*see* Housetonic)

Stoney (*see* Assiniboin)

Supai (*see* Havasupai)

Sushwap
Geographic Region: Great Basin (southern British Columbia)
Linguistic Group: Salishan
Principal Dwelling Type:
    Semisubterranean house
Principal Subsistence Type: Fish, large game

Above: **A present-day Sioux celebrates his heritage in one of the many pow wows and festivals held in South Dakota throughout the summer.**

Susquehannock (Conestoga, Meherrin)
Geographic Region: Northeast (eastern shore of Chesapeake Bay and eastern Pennsylvania)
Linguistic Group: Iroquoian
Principal Dwelling Type:
  Rectangular barrel-roofed house
Principal Subsistence Type: Maize

When they were first encountered by John Smith in 1608, he described the Susquehannock as 'the most noble and heroic nation of Indians that dwell upon the confines of America.' The tribe formed early friendships with the Dutch and the Swedes, as well as the English. Although related to the five nations of the Iroquois League, the Susquehannock carried out constant warfare against them. The Susquehannock War of 1673 was the beginning of the downfall of the tribe, who were almost completely destroyed by the Iroquois by 1675. The few survivors joined the Nottoway and later formed a new tribe called Meherrin, which disappeared by 1700. They reappeared shortly thereafter under the name Conestoga, in honor of their ancient village. By 1763 their number had dwindled to 20, after which the last few were massacred by a party of rioters, known as the Paxton Boys, who were angered by a war being waged by another tribe.

Swallah
Geographic Region: Northwest Coast (Puget Sound, Washington)
Linguistic Group: Salishan
Principal Dwelling Type:
  Rectangular plank house
Principal Subsistence Type: Fish

Swinomish
Geographic Region: Northwest Coast (Puget Sound, Washington)
Linguistic Group: Salishan
Principal Dwelling Type:
  Rectangular plank house
Principal Subsistence Type: Fish

In 1970 there were 364 Swinomish living in Washington, and in 1985 there were 624 people on the Swinomish Reservation.

Below: A Sioux Ghost Dance ceremonial shirt. The Ghost Dance religion developed among the Plains Indians in the 1890s at the peak of their frustration with whites. During the dance, participants worked themselves into a frenzy and could envision a future of Indian supremacy.

Taensa
Geographic Region: Southeast
(lower Mississippi valley)
Linguistic Group: Muskogean-Taensa
(extinct, never recorded)
Principal Dwelling Type:
Rectangular thatched house
Principal Subsistence Type: Maize

Tagish
Geographic Region: Subarctic
(coastal mountains, Alaska and British
Columbia)
Linguistic Group: Algonquian-Nadene
Principal Dwelling Type: Double lean-to
Principal Subsistence Type: Fish

Tahitan
Geographic Region: Subarctic
(coastal mountains, Alaska and British
Columbia)
Linguistic Group: Athapascan
Principal Dwelling Type: Double lean-to
Principal Subsistence Type:
Caribou, moose

Taidnapam
Geographic Region: Northwest Coast
(south-central Washington)
Linguistic Group: Salishan
Principal Dwelling Type:
Rectangular plank house
Principal Subsistence Type: Fish

Takamiut (Baffin Island Eskimo, *see*
Eskimo)

Takelma
Geographic Region: Northwest Coast
(southern Oregon)
Linguistic Group: Penutian-Takelma
Principal Dwelling Type:
Semisubterranean house
Principal Subsistence Type: Mix of animal and wild plant foods

Tamaroa (*see* Illinois)

Tanaina
Geographic Region: Subarctic (south-central Alaska)
Linguistic Group: Athapascan
Principal Dwelling Type: Rectangular
earth-covered Alaskan house

Principal Subsistence Type:
Caribou, moose, fish
Note: Not to be confused with Tanana,
also from Alaska

Tanana (Nabesna)
Geographic Region: Subarctic (Yukon
and Kuskokwin rivers, central Alaska)
Linguistic Group: Athapascan
Principal Dwelling Type: Rectangular
earth-covered Alaskan house
Principal Subsistence Type:
Caribou, moose, fish
The Tanana Chiefs Conference (TCC)
group of the Fairbanks Agency in Alaska
had a population of 7039 in 1985. The
Tanana are not to be confused with the
Tanaina, who are also from Alaska.

Taos Pueblo (*see* Pueblo)

Taskigi (*see* Tuskogee)

Tawakoni, Tawehash (*see* Wichita)

Tegesta (*see* Seminole)

Tenino
Geographic Region: Northwest Coast
Linguistic Group: Penutian-Sahaptin
Principal Dwelling Type: Conical tipi
Principal Subsistence Type: Mix of animal and wild plant foods

Tesuque Pueblo (*see* Pueblo)

Teton Sioux (*see* **Sioux**)

Thlingchadinne (*see* Dogrib)

Thompson
Geographic Region: Great Basin
Linguistic Group: Salishan
Principal Dwelling Type:
Semisubterranean house
Principal Subsistence Type:
Caribou, moose, fish

Tillamook
Geographic Region: Northwest Coast
(northwestern Oregon coast)
Linguistic Group: Salishan
Principal Dwelling Type:
Rectangular plank house
Principal Subsistence Type: Fish

Timiquan (*see* Seminole)

Tinde (*see* Apache)

Tionontati (*see* Tobacco)

Tipai
Geographic Region: California

Linguistic Group: Hokan
Principal Dwelling Type: Domed bark,
thatch or hide house
Principal Subsistence Type: Wild plants,
small game

Tlingit (Kolash, Kaluschian, Tlinkit)
Geographic Region: Northwest Coast
(southern Alaska)
Linguistic Group: Algonquian-Nadene
(Tlingit)
Principal Dwelling Type:
Rectangular plank house
Principal Subsistence Type: Fish
Subgroups: Prince William Sound—
Tongass, Yakutat
Alexander Archipelago—Auk, Chilkat, Henya, Hoonah, Hootznahoo,
Kake, Killisnoo, Kuiu, Sanya, Sitka
and Stikine

The Tlingit were the northernmost of
the major tribes of the Northwest Coast.
They were the dominant tribe in the Alaskan panhandle, and had many characteristics in common with such tribes as the
Haida and Kwakiutl. These included a
highly developed religion and social structure, which included the potlatch ceremony *(see also* Haida and Kwakiutl). The
Tlingit were organized into clans that
were associated with birds or animals such
as the raven, eagle or wolf. Fishing was an
extremely important activity for the Tlingit, as it was for the other tribes of the
region, and salmon formed the staple of
their diet. For their fishing expeditions,
the Tlingit carved huge cedar log ships
that often measured 60 feet or more. They
were also skilled wood carvers and basket
makers.

The Russians were the earliest white
men to establish permanent settlements in
Alaska. The first major conflict between
the Russians and the Tlingit came in 1793
when Alexander Baronov sailed into
Yschugat Bay. Baronov's ship was attacked by a heavily armed Tlingit raiding
party, and in the ensuing battle two Russians and nine of their Aleut crewmen
were killed. The Tlingit lost 12 men, despite the fact that they were wearing
wooden helmets and armor that reportedly was heavy enough to be able to turn
away bullets.

Baronov wanted to establish Russian
influence throughout the region between
Kodiak and Sitka where there were Russian outposts, but he was generally unsuccessful in negotiations with the Tlingit. In
1799 the Tlingit intercepted a Russian expedition near Sitka, killing 26. In 1802 the
Tlingit attacked and captured the Russian
fort at Sitka and held it for two years. The
Russians were able to recapture it in 1804

Above: **Two Tlingit girls, Tsacotna and Natsanitna, pose for a photograph in 1903. The nose rings are common ornaments among Indians of the Northwestern tribes, jewelry being a symbol of status.**

only with the support of the big guns aboard the frigate *Neva,* which was brought in for the battle. Later in 1804 the Tlingit attacked and captured the Russian outpost at Yakutat.

The year 1834 saw the arrival of missionary Ivan Veniaminov, who took the time to learn the Tlingit language, something few Russians had been willing to do.

He is credited with saving a large number of Tlingit during the 1836 smallpox epidemic. When he was promoted to bishop in 1841, Veniaminov decreed that the Tlingit and other tribes that had not been converted 'shall be permitted to carry on their devotions according to their own rites.' He instructed his priests to convert the Indians only through logical persuasion, 'in no case resorting to coercion.'

When Veniaminov returned to Russia in 1854, relations between the Russians and Tlingit once again turned sour, and later in the year the Indians attacked the

port of New Archangel, but were driven off. In October 1867 the Tlingit watched the formalities from their canoes in the harbor as New Archangel was transferred, along with all of Alaska, to the United States. Relations between the Tlingit and the Americans were hardly better than they had been with the Russians. The US Army was withdrawn in 1877 without the US government having worked out a policy regarding the Tlingit. In the years to follow, the white settlers gave the Tlingit wide berth for fear of sparking the violence that had plagued the Russians.

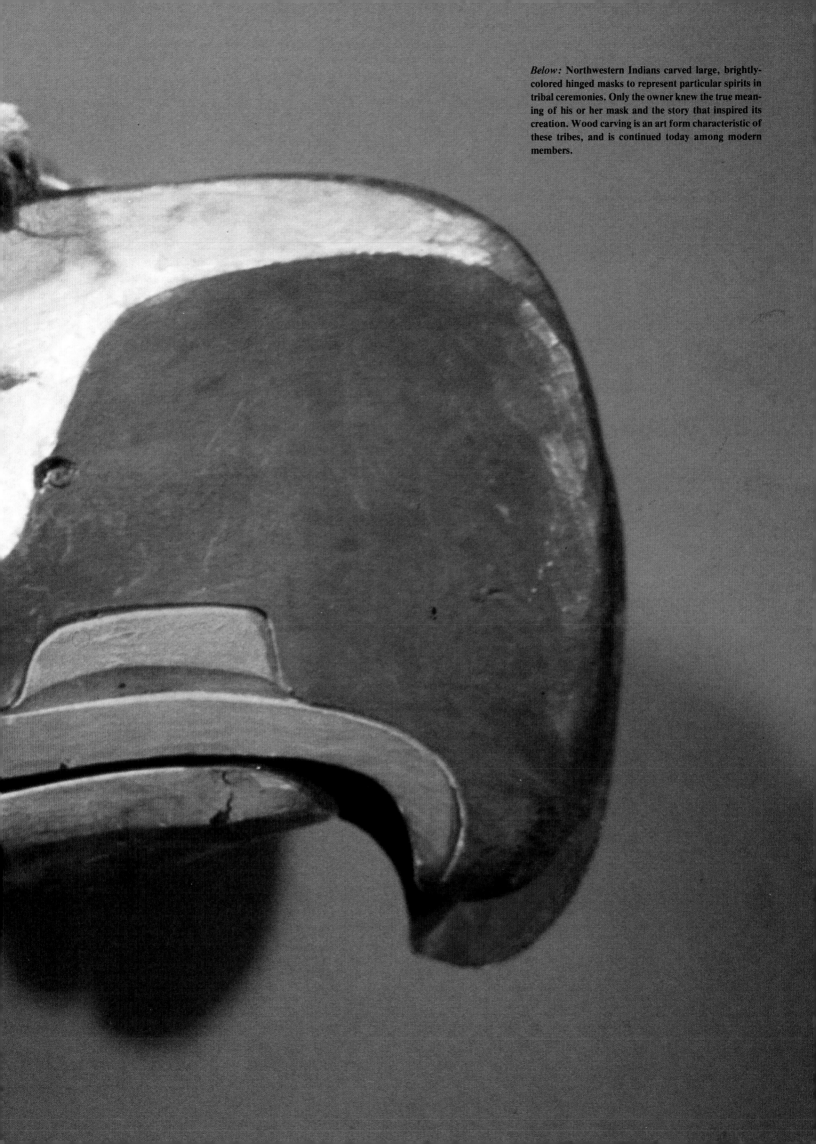

Below: Northwestern Indians carved large, brightly-colored hinged masks to represent particular spirits in tribal ceremonies. Only the owner knew the true meaning of his or her mask and the story that inspired its creation. Wood carving is an art form characteristic of these tribes, and is continued today among modern members.

With the Alaska gold rush of the 1880s, the economic life of the Tlingit changed dramatically. Some of them worked in the mines and still others hired out with their big canoes to haul freight, underselling the white boat operators and still turning a profit. The Indians, however, were not allowed to file mining claims until 1931.

As the twentieth century arrived in Alaska, the Tlingit found themselves generally unimpeded in their traditional practices of religion, language and potlatch, nor had they ever been forced onto a reservation. On the other hand, the US government had never addressed the legal question of whether they were citizens. It was not until 1924 that the question of allowing the Tlingit to vote came up, and they finally were allowed to legally cast ballots. In 1926 a Tlingit leader named William Paull was elected to the Alaska Territorial Legislature, and in 1953 the Tlingit and Haida formed the joint Haida-Tlingit Land Claims Council.

In 1970 the Tlingit population in Alaska numbered 6063, and in 1985 it numbered approximately 8700.

Tobacco (Petun, Tionontati)
Geographic Region: Northeast (west of Lake Huron)
Linguistic Group: Iroquoian
Principal Dwelling Type: Domed bark, thatch or hide house
Principal Subsistence Type: Maize

Like many tribes of the region, the Tobacco also cultivated the smoking substance for which they were named. Tobacco was widely grown by North American Indians and used for both ceremonial and medicinal purposes.

Tocabago (*see* Seminole)

Tolowa
Geographic Region: Northwestern California
Linguistic Group: Athapascan
Principal Dwelling Type: Rectangular plank house
Principal Subsistence Type: Mix of animal and wild plant foods

Tongass (*see* Tlingit)

Tonkawa
Geographic Region: Southeast (eastern Texas)
Linguistic Group: Algonquian (Tonkawan group)

Principal Dwelling Type: Domed thatched house
Principal Subsistence Type: Hunting, maize

The Tonkawa name is derived from the Waco term *tonkaweya,* meaning 'they all stick together.' In the eighteenth century, they were allied with the Comanche and Wichita against the Apache, but the situation was reversed in the following century. The Tonkawa were also hostile to the Spanish, and early attempts by Spanish missionaries to convert the Tonkawa were abandoned in 1756. Frequent warfare and epidemics severely weakened the tribe and in October 1862 they were badly defeated by the Caddo, Shawnee, Wichita and Delaware. In 1884, after temporary resettlement near Fort Griffin, Texas, they were assigned a reservation in Indian Territory. By 1905 they were reported to be prosperous farmers, and in 1907 they became citizens of Oklahoma.

In 1778 the French indicated a possible Tonkawa population of 1500, which was reduced to half that number by 1847. In 1890 there were 73 Tonkawa, and in 1910 there were 53. The Indian census of 1944 indicated 56 Tonkawa still in Oklahoma.

Tonto Apache (*see* Apache)

Tosawi (*see* Shoshone)

Towiache (*see* Wichita)

Trinity Wintun (*see* Wintun)

Tsetseu
Geographic Region: Subarctic (interior mountains, Alaska and Yukon)
Linguistic Group: Athapascan
Principal Dwelling Type: Double lean-to
Principal Subsistence Type: Caribou, moose

Tsimshian
Geographic Region: Northwest Coast (northern British Columbia)
Linguistic Group: Penutian-Tsimshian
Principal Dwelling Type: Rectangular plank house
Subgroup: Nishga

The Tsimshian were traditionally located between the Nass and Skeena rivers and on adjacent islands. While fish, particularly salmon, formed their dietary staple, the Tsimshian also hunted bear and deer in the interior. They were culturally related to the Haida and Tlingit, sharing with them such aspects of Northwest Coast life as shamanic religion and totemic art. However, they were not nearly as warlike as the Tlingit.

In 1857 some members of the tribe at Metlakatla were organized into a model Christian community by William Duncan, a Scottish lay preacher. When the British attempted to put the tribe on a reservation in 1887, a group of Tsimshian leaders went to England to ask for the return of their lands. In a prepared statement they told Queen Victoria:

What we don't like about this government is their saying this: we will give you this much land. We cannot understand it. They have never bought it from our forefathers. They have never fought and conquered our people and taken the land that way, and yet they now say they will give us so much land—our own land.

The British government took no action and the Tsimshian formed a Land Committee to hire lawyers to draw up a petition. Their position was presented to the Imperial Privy Council in 1913, but again no action was taken. In 1927 they were turned down on their land claim and forbidden to take further legal action. In 1951 the Revised Indian Act reversed much of the anti-Indian legislation of previous years, and made it possible for the Tsimshian to once again pursue their legal claim to their land.

In 1967 the Tsimshian tribal population stood at 1706.

Tsoya'ha (*see* Yuchi)

Tubatulabal
Geographic Region: California (Kern River, Sierra Nevada)
Linguistic Group: Uto-Aztecan
Principal Dwelling Type: Crude conical tipi
Principal Subsistence Type: Acorns

Tukabahchee (*see* Creek)

Tukaduka (*see* Shoshone)

Tunica
Geographic Region: Southeast (Mississippi valley)
Linguistic Group: Algonquian
Principal Dwelling Type: Rectangular thatched house
Principal Subsistence Type: Hunting, maize

Tuscarora
Geographic Region: Southeast (eastern North Carolina)
Linguistic Group: Iroquoian
Principal Dwelling Type: Rectangular barrel-roofed house
Principal Subsistence Type: Maize

Opposite: A Chilkat dress woven by Indians of the Northwest coast from a yarn mixture of cedar-bark fiber and mountain goat wool. The natural white material was then dyed for color. The garment is a sign of wealth and was usually comissioned by a father or husband, who provided the design. *Right:* A Tlingit carving. Note the figure's painted mask and nose ring.

The name Tuscarora is derived from the Iroquoian *skarúre,* signifying 'hemp gatherers.' When the white man arrived on their lands in 1708, they were organized into 15 towns and had about 1200 men under arms. Three years later, in the face of white encroachment, these warriors began raiding the white settlements, killing many people. After two years of warfare, the Tuscarora were defeated by volunteers brought in from South Carolina and the remaining members of the tribe moved north to join the Iroquois League in New York. In 1846 the Tuscarora were removed to Indian Territory, where they numbered 32 in 1906 at the time of Oklahoma statehood. In 1970 those still remaining in New York numbered 650, up from 225 in 1950. In 1985 the population of the Tuscarora Reservation in New York was 793.

Tuskogee (Taskigi, Tuskegee)
Geographic Region: Southeast (Alabama)
Linguistic Group: Muskogean
Principal Dwelling Type:
   Rectangular thatched house
Principal Subsistence Type: Maize
   The Tuskogee name derives from the Creek word *tv'seki'yv,* meaning 'one who has received a war name.' When first encountered by De Soto in 1540, the tribe was living in northern Alabama along the Tennessee and Tallapoosa rivers. Eventually the former joined the Cherokee tribe and the latter joined the Creek confederacy, where they were known as the Upper Creek. When the Creek were moved to Indian Territory, the Tuskogee moved with them as part of the Creek Nation. Tuskogee Town was one of the largest towns in the Creek Nation, with an 1891 population of 401.

Tutchone
Geographic Region: Subarctic
   (coastal mountains, Alaska and British
   Columbia)
Linguistic Group: Athapascan
Principal Dwelling Type: Double lean-to,
   rectangular plank house
Principal Subsistence Type:
   Caribou, moose, fish

Tutelo
Geographic Region: Southeast (western
   Virginia)

Linguistic Group: Siouan
Principal Dwelling Type:
   Rectangular barrel-roofed house
Principal Subsistence Type: Maize

Twana
Geographic Region: Northwest Coast
   (southwestern Washington)
Linguistic Group: Salishan
Principal Dwelling Type:
   Rectangular plank house
Principal Subsistence Type: Fish

Twightwee (*see* Miami)

Two Kettle (*see* Sioux)

Tygh Valley
Geographic Region: Great Basin (central
   Oregon along Columbia River)
Linguistic Group: Penutian-Sahaptin
Principal Dwelling Type: Crude conical
   tipi
Principal Subsistence Type: Mix of
   animal and wild plant foods

Below: The interior of chief **Dlart-Reech's** house, around 1895. The Tlingit were great traders, and accumulation of possessions determined a person's status within the tribe.

Below: A Uinta Ute warrior and his bride, photographed in 1874 in northwest Utah. Normally, Ute couples lived with or near the woman's family. The tribe was nomadic, moving to the mountains during the summer and back into the Great Basin Valley for the winter in a seasonal search for food. Many of the smaller reservations today are located in this area.

Uchee (*see* Yuchi)

Umatilla
Geographic Region: Great Basin (northeastern Oregon)
Linguistic Group: Penutian-Sahaptin
Principal Dwelling Type: Crude conical tipi, semisubterranean house
Principal Subsistence Type: Mix of animal and wild plant foods

The Umatilla are still living near the Columbia River gorge in northeastern Oregon, where they were located when first visited by Lewis and Clark in 1804. In 1950 they numbered 1150, and in 1985 the Umatilla Agency and Reservation had a population of 1578.

Umpqua
Geographic Region: Northwest Coast (central Oregon coast)
Linguistic Group: Penutian-Umpqua
Principal Dwelling Type:
Rectangular plank house
Principal Subsistence Type: Fish

Unalachtigo (*see* Delaware)

Unaligmiut (West Alaskan Eskimo, *see* Eskimo)

Unami (*see* Delaware)

Upper Creek (*see* Tuskogee)

Ute (Cumumbah, Pahvant, Quon-di-ats)
Geographic Region: Great Basin (western Colorado, eastern Utah, northern New Mexico)
Linguistic Group: Uto-Aztecan
Principal Dwelling Type: Crude conical tipi
Principal Subsistence Type: Large game

The Ute were related to the Bannock and Gosiute tribes, as well as the larger Paiute and Shoshone groups, and a considerable amount of intermixing took place. Because of these relationships, the Ute are considered a Great Basin tribe, although their proximity to the Plains meant that they had many cultural traits in common with the Plains tribes. Like the Plains tribes, and unlike many typical Basin tribes such as the Paiute, the Ute

"Mrs Moses Johnson"
Umatilla Tribe
MnJ. Moorhouse

Above and Opposite: **Although a century separates these two Umatilla women, Mrs Moses Johnson (*left*) and this young lady (*right*) who was photographed in 1986, cultural pride and heritage are of a timeless quality. The custom of braiding one's** hair into two long plaits continues to be popular, even though clothing styles have changed from elaborately-embroidered cloth to jeans and T-shirts. The younger woman is watching the Chief Joseph Days parade, shown in the photograph on page 6.

hunted big game such as deer and antelope. They were involved in sporadic warfare against the Spanish in the eighteenth century and against the Americans in the nineteenth century, until they were finally placed on reservations in the 1880s. The state of Utah, which joined the Union in 1896, is named for the tribe.

In 1970 the Ute population stood at 3557, up from 1000 in 1950. In 1985 there were 2427 people at the Southern Ute and Ute Mountain reservations, and 2270 at the Uintah-Ouray Reservation in Utah.

Utukokmiut (North Alaskan Eskimo, *see* Eskimo)

Wabunaki (*see* Abnaki)

Waco (Honeches, Houeches, Huanchane)
Geographic Region: Plains and Prairies (eastern Texas)
Linguistic Group: Caddoan

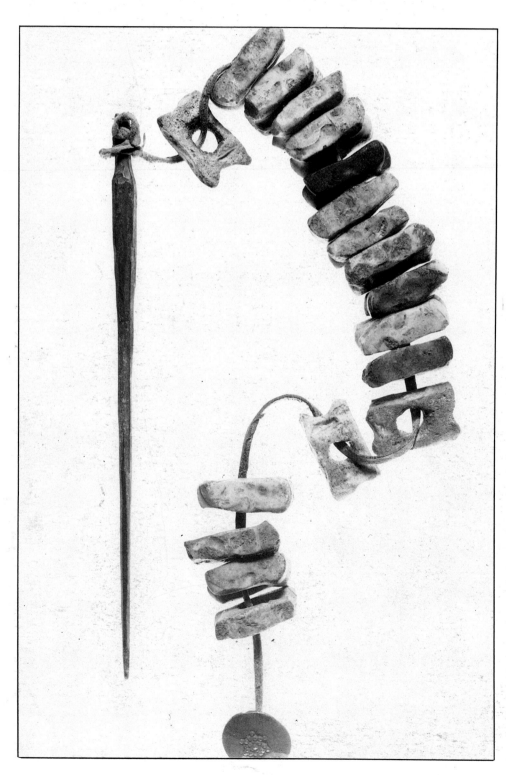

Principal Dwelling Type:
Domed thatched house
Principal Subsistence Type:
Hunting, maize

The Waco were living on the Arkansas River in Oklahoma when first contacted by the French in 1719, but by 1779 they had migrated into the Brazos River country of Texas. They were removed to a reservation in Indian Territory in 1859, where they were associated with the Wichita and later the Wichita-Caddo Reservation. In 1859 the Waco numbered 114, and, although they gradually merged with the larger tribes, there were still 37 Waco living in Indian Territory in 1894.

Wahkiakim (*see* Chinook)

Wahpekute Sioux (*see* Sioux)

Wahpeton Sioux (*see* Sioux)

Wahunsonacock (*see* Powhatan)

Wailaki
Geographic Region:
Northwestern California
Linguistic Group: Athapascan
Principal Dwelling Type:
Rectangular plank house
Principal Subsistence Type: Mix of animal and wild plant foods

Walapai
Geographic Region: Southwest
Linguistic Group: Hokan-Yuman
Principal Dwelling Type: Domed bark, thatch or hide house
Principal Subsistence Type: Wild plants, small game

Walla Walla
Geographic Region: Great Basin (Columbia River region)
Linguistic Group: Penutian-Sahaptin
Principal Dwelling Type:
Semisubterranean house
Principal Subsistence Type: Fish

Walua
Geographic Region: Great Basin (eastern Washington)
Linguistic Group: Sahaptin
Principal Dwelling Type:
Semisubterranean house
Principal Subsistence Type: Fish, game

Left: **The deer bone game, popular with California's Wailaki people.** *Top right:* **Massasoit, chief of the Wampanoags, ruled much of the land in the Northeast desired by the English. In a treaty with Captain John Smith in 1621, he shared land with the English.** *Bottom right:* **Governor John Carver accepts the peace pipe offered to him by Massasoit.**

Wampanoag (Pokanoket)

Geographic Region: Northeast (Narragansett Bay area)

Linguistic Group: Algonquian

Principal Dwelling Type:
 Rectangular barrel-roofed house

Principal Subsistence Type: Fish, cultivated plants

The now extinct Wampanoag were living in 30 villages in eastern Massachusetts at the time of the arrival of the Pilgrims in 1620. The Wampanoag chief, Massasoit, was particularly friendly to the Pilgrims and other early white settlers, giving them food and assistance. He died in 1661 and was succeeded by Chief Wamsotta, who died the following year. Wamsotta was succeeded as chief, or sachem, by his brother, Metacomet, who came to be known to the English as 'King Philip.' In 1674 a Christian Wampanoag named Sansamon was murdered by other Indians, who in turn were executed by the English. Indian reprisals led the English to drive Philip and his people off Indian land. King Philip and the Wampanoag joined the Nipmuck in central Massachusetts, and in 1675 began the bloody two years of

warfare known and King Philip's War. During the war no fewer than 12 English towns were completely destroyed, including Brookfield and Deerfield in 1675, and Lancaster and Bridgewater the following year. The Narragansett joined the fray and were beaten by the colonists. The Nipmuck were also defeated, and on 12 August 1676 King Philip himself was tracked down and killed at Mount Hope, Rhode Island. The remaining Wampanoag joined the Narragansett tribe in the wake of their resounding defeat.

Wanapam
Geographic Region:
Great Basin (Washington)
Linguistic Group: Penutian-Sahaptin
Principal Dwelling Type:
Semisubterranean house
Principal Subsistence Type: Fish, large game

Wappinger
Geographic Region: Northeast (New York, lower Hudson River)
Linguistic Group: Algonquian
Principal Dwelling Type:
Rectangular barrel-roofed house
Principal Subsistence Type:
Hunting, fish, maize

Wappo
Geographic Region: California (north of San Francisco Bay)
Linguistic Group: Penutian
Principal Dwelling Type: Crude conical tipi
Principal Subsistence Type: Acorns

Wasco
Geographic Region: Great Basin (north-central Oregon)
Linguistic Group: Penutian-Chinook
Principal Dwelling Type:
Semisubterranean house
Principal Subsistence Type: Fish

Washoe (Washo)
Geographic Region: Great Basin (Lake Tahoe area)
Linguistic Group: Hokan
Principal Dwelling Type: Crude conical tipi
Principal Subsistence Type: Wild plants, small game, fish
In 1985 there were 463 Washoe at the Carson and Dresslerville colonies in Nevada, and 203 at the Woodfords Colony in California.

Wauyukma
Geographic Region: Great Basin (eastern Washington)

Below: Wintun Joe and his wife, photographed in 1903 at the McCloud Reservation near Redding in northern California. He was 95 years old at the time. According to local tribal members, he was given Thomas as a last name after saying the Wintun word 'tome' which means to tell the truth. He earned the name many years earlier while being questioned about a robbery at Old Shasta.

Linguistic Group: Sahaptin
Principal Dwelling Type:
  Semisubterranean house
Principal Subsistence Type: Fish, game

Wawyachtonoc (*see* Mahican, Wea)

Wazhazhe (*see* Osage)

Wea
Geographic Region: Northeast (Illinois,
  Indiana)
Linguistic Group: Algonquian
Principal Dwelling Type: Domed bark,
  thatch or hide house
Principal Subsistence Type: Maize

The name Wea is derived from the Algonquian *Wayah-tonuki,* meaning 'people of the round channel.' This may mean that they are related to the Wawy-achtonoc, the Algonquian-speaking Mahican subgroup whose name means the same. The French first visited the Wea in 1718 at Oviatenon (Weatenon?), their village on the Wabash River, where they grew extensive fields of maize and pumpkins. Relations were good with the French, who set up a trading post nearby. In 1757 the Wea and Piankashaw attempted to establish equally good relations with the English, but were swept up in the conflict between the two European powers.

In 1791 the Wea villages on the Wabash were destroyed by the white settlers, and in 1818 they sold the last of their lands. In 1832 they settled with the Piankashaw in Kansas, with whom they became confederated in 1854. In 1867 they were removed to Indian Territory, where they were merged with the larger Peoria group.

Wenatchi
Geographic Region: Great Basin (central
  Washington along Columbia River)
Linguistic Group: Salishan
Principal Dwelling Type:
  Semisubterranean house
Principal Subsistence Type: Fish
Note: The Wenatchi National Forest was
  named after the tribe.

Wesort (Brandywine)
Geographic Region:
  Northeast (Maryland)
Linguistic Group: Algonquian
Principal Dwelling Type:
  Rectangular barrel-roofed house
Principal Subsistence Type: Maize

West Alaskan Eskimo (*see* Eskimo)

Right and Opposite: Yuki Indians in dance costume.
The headdresses are made of magpie feathers.

Western Apache (*see* Apache)

West Greenland Eskimo (*see* Eskimo)

Wheelappa (*see* Kwalhioqua)

White Mountain Apache (*see* Apache)

Wichita (Ousita, Panis, Tawakoni, Tawe-
hash, Towiache, Wusita)
Geographic Region: Plains and Prairies
(Oklahoma, Texas)
Linguistic Group: Caddoan
Principal Dwelling Type:
Domed thatched house
Principal Subsistence Type: Maize
The Wichita name is derived from the
Choctaw *wia chitoh,* meaning 'big arbor'
or 'big platform.' They were originally
agricultural people living in the Arkansas,
Brazos and Red rivers country, where
they grew corn and pumpkins that they
traded to the Plains hunters for buffalo.
They were allied with the Waco and
Kichai and at odds with the Apache and
Osage. In 1746, with some careful persua-
sion from the French, the Wichita became
allied with their former enemies, the
Comanche, in warfare against the Apache
and Osage. A burgeoning trade relationship between the Wichita and Comanche
also benefited the French traders in the
region.
In 1834 US Army Colonel Henry
Dodge arrived in the area and helped
mediate an end to the conflict between the
Wichita and Osage. Relations between the
Wichita and the United States were good
until 1858, when a Wichita encampment
in Oklahoma was the subject of an unprovoked, nighttime surprise attack by
US troops who had mistaken them for
Comanche. A year of warfare ensued,
which left the tribe with their crops destroyed and many of their people dead.
They were placed on a reservation, where
they remained until the Civil War forced
them to Indian Territory as refugees.
They returned in 1867, and in 1873 the assassination of Chief Isadowa by the Osage
nearly led to war. In 1894 the Wichita
land in Indian Territory was divided
among 965 members of the tribe. In 1985
the population of the Wichita tribe in
Oklahoma stood at 608, up from 460 in
1970.

Willopah (*see* Kwalhioqua)

Wind River (*see* Shoshone)

Winnebago
Geographic Region: Northeast (western
shore of Lake Michigan)

Linguistic Group: Siouan-Chiewere
Principal Dwelling Type: Domed bark,
thatch or hide house
Principal Subsistence Type:
Hunting, maize
When first encountered by the French
in 1634, the Winnebago were living in
the Green Bay region, surrounded by
Algonquian-speaking peoples. Legend
has it that they were once a much larger
tribe in the region but that they almost
had been annihilated by the powerful Illinois. The Winnebago had good relations
with the French, and later the British, but
resisted the American settlers when they
began moving into the region in the late
eighteenth century. In 1827 they initiated
the Winnebago War and were defeated.
Between 1828 and 1840 they ceded all
their lands in Wisconsin and were removed to Minnesota.
The Winnebago are said to have numbered 5800 in 1822, but the Winnebago
War and the 1832 smallpox epidemic reduced their population by about 25 percent. In 1970 there were 1813 Winnebago
in Nebraska and 1330 descendants of
those members of the tribe who had returned to Wisconsin. In 1985 the Winnebago Reservation in Nebraska had a
population of 1183 and the Wisconsin
Winnebago tribe numbered 1912.

Wintun (Winta)
Geographic Region: California (Mt
Shasta and upper Sacramento River
region)
Linguistic Group: Penutian-Wintun
Principal Dwelling Type: Domed bark,
thatch or hide house
Principal Subsistence Type:
Hunting, maize
Subgroups: Hill Wintun, Northern Win-
tun (Wintu or Trinity Wintun), River
Wintun
The aboriginal population of the Win-

tun is estimated to have stood at 9800,
including 5300 Wintu. In 1970 there were
still 179 Wintun in California. In 1985
there were 101 people at the Cortina
Rancheria, 72 at the Colusa Rancheria,
133 at the Grindstone Rancheria, and 49
at the Rumsey Rancheria.

Wiyot
Geographic Region: Northern California
(Blue Lake)
Linguistic Group:
Algonquian-Wiyot (language isolate)
Principal Dwelling Type:
Rectangular plank house
Principal Subsistence Type: Mix of
animal and wild plant foods, fish

Wusita (*see* Wichita)

Wyandot (Huron)
Geographic Region: Northeast (northeast
of Lake Huron)
Linguistic Group: Iroquoian
Principal Dwelling Type:
Rectangular barrel-roofed house
Principal Subsistence Type: Maize
The name Wyandot (or Wendat) is Iroquoian for 'people of the peninsula,' a
reference to a peninsula in southern
Ontario east of Lake Huron where they
originally lived. Their population was
estimated at 20,000 in 1615 when first
encountered by the French under Samuel
de Champlain, who referred to them as
Huron ('bristly-headed ruffian'). The
first Wyandot groups in the region probably arrived in the early fourteenth century. In addition to maize, the Wyandot
raised beans, squash, sunflowers and
tobacco.
The arrival of the white man on the
East Coast pushed the tribes of the Iroquois League farther west and into conflict with the Wyandot. A strong rivalry
developed between the two Iroquoian-
speaking tribes over the issue of control of
the fur trade in the upper Great Lakes
region. In a key battle that took place in
1649, the Wyandot were nearly annihilated by the more powerful Iroquois. The
descendants of the tribe survive today as
the Hurons of Lorette in Quebec and the
Wyandot tribe in Oklahoma. The respective populations of these two groups were
1273 and 494 in 1984.

Wynochee
Geographic Region: Northwest Coast
(Washington coast)
Linguistic Group: Salishan
Principal Dwelling Type:
Rectangular plank house
Principal Subsistence Type: Fish

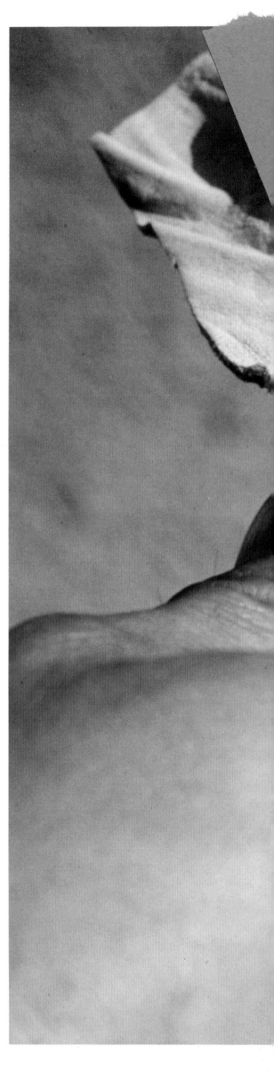

Yahi

Geographic Region: California (northern Sacramento River valley)
Linguistic Group: Hokan
Principal Dwelling Type:
   Semisubterranean house
Principal Subsistence Type: Mix of animal and wild plant foods

The Yahi and Yana were related tribes that once had an estimated total population of 3820, but which are now extinct.

Yakima

Geographic Region: Great Basin (Columbia River region)
Linguistic Group: Penutian-Sahaptin
Principal Dwelling Type: Bark and skin long-house
Principal Subsistence Type: Fish

The Yakima were closely related to the Nez Percé, both linguistically and culturally. They did not engage in agriculture but lived on roots, berries and nuts and fish taken from the Columbia River. They met Lewis and Clark on the Columbia in 1804.

In 1855 an attempt by the US government to place the Yakima on a reservation led to open warfare. Under the leadership of Chief Kamiakin, they held out for three years before they were defeated.

In 1970 the Yakima Reservation in Washington, near the city named for the tribe, had a population of 5391, up from 3370 in 1950. In 1985 there were 7987 people at the Yakima Agency and Reservation.

Yamasee

Geographic Region: Southeast (eastern South Carolina)
Linguistic Group: Muskogean
Principal Dwelling type:
   Rectangular thatched house
Principal Subsistence Type: Maize

Prompted by Spanish and English encroachment on their land, the Yamasee initiated the Yamasee War in 1715. On 15 April they massacred 90 traders and their families. This forced Spanish and English retaliation, which drove the tribe south into Florida, where they became integrated into the Seminole tribe.

Yana

Geographic Region: California (northeastern Sacramento River valley to Mt Shasta)
Linguistic Group: Hokan
Principal Dwelling Type:
   Semisubterranean house
Principal Subsistence Type: Mix of animal and wild plant foods

The Yana and Yahi were related tribes that once had an estimated total population of 1830, but which are now extinct.

Yankton Sioux, Yantonai Sioux (*see* Sioux)

Below: **Glass arrow points made by Ishi, the last member of the Yahi tribe, using the method at *right*.**

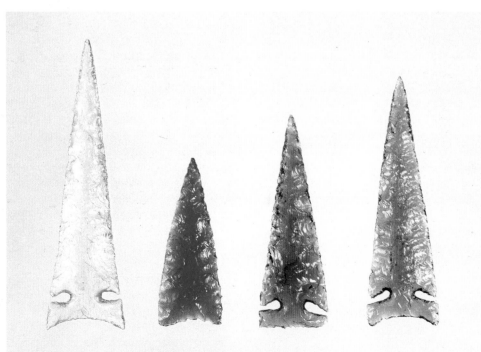

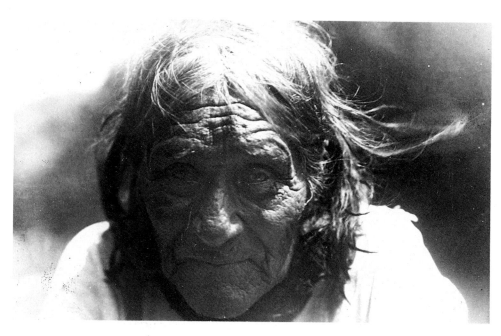

Yaquina

Geographic Region: Northwest Coast (central Oregon coast)
Linguistic Group: Penutian
Principal Dwelling Type:
   Rectangular plank house
Principal Subsistence Type: Fish

Yavapai

Geographic Region: Southwest
Linguistic Group: Hokan-Yuman
Principal Dwelling Type: Crude conical tipi
Principal Subsistence Type: Wild plants, small game

Yaqui

Geographic Region: Southwest (Arizona, Sonora)
Linguistic Group: Cahitan (Uto-Aztecan)
Principal Dwelling Type: Domed bark, thatch or hide house
Principal Subsistence Type: Maize

The Yaqui were once located near the Yaqui River of Sonora, Mexico, but migrated north into Arizona. Although they had been surrounded by the Spanish since the sixteenth century, the Yaqui were never subdued by them. They revolted against the Spanish in 1740 and 1764, and were frequently in conflict with the Mexican government after 1825. From 1885 to 1906 hostilities were almost continuous, and toward the end of the war, many were removed to southern Mexico. In 1915 they were at war with Pancho Villa in the Yaqui Valley, and in 1916 they killed 200 Mexican troops.

Yellowknife

Geographic Region: Subarctic (south of Great Slave Lake, MacKenzie Territory)
Linguistic Group: Athapascan
Principal Dwelling Type: Crude conical tipi
Principal Subsistence Type:
   Caribou, moose

In 1967 there were 466 Yellowknife in Canada.

Yokuts

Geographic Region: California (San Joaquin River Valley)
Linguistic Group: Penutian-Yokuts
Principal Dwelling Type: Domed bark, thatch or hide house
Principal Subsistence Type: Acorns

In 1970 there were 504 Yokuts in California.

Ysa (*see* Catawba)

Yuchi (Choya'ha, Euchee, Tsoya'ha, Uchee)

Geographic Region: Southeast (Georgia)
Linguistic Group: Hokan-Siouan
Principal Dwelling Type:
   Rectangular thatched house
Principal Subsistence Type: Maize

The Yuchi name originated from the Hitchiti term *ochesse,* meaning 'people of another language.' However, the Yuchi referred to themselves as Choya'ha or Tsoya'ha, which mean 'children of the sun.' In 1540 De Soto reported their name as Chisca. The tribe probably preceded the Creek into the southeast and later joined the Creek confederacy as a means of defense against the encroachment of white settlement. In 1677 the Yuchi suffered defeat at the hands of the Spanish, and in 1682 some members of the tribe were recorded as living in Illinois. In the eighteenth century other Yuchi became identified with the Shawnee and the Upper Creeks in the Tallapoosa River Country, where the Yuchi fought alongside them in the Creek War of 1813–14.

After the Civil War, which had seen Yuchi associated with both sides, the tribe relocated to the Creek Nation in Indian Territory in 1867. The Creek constitution of that year provided for Yuchi representation on the Creek National Council.

In 1891 the Creek Nation Council counted 580 Yuchi, and by 1949 that number increased to 1216.

Yuki

Geographic Region: California (north of San Francisco Bay)
Linguistic Group; Hokan-Yuki
Principal Dwelling Type:
   Rectangular plank house
Principal Subsistence Type: Mix of animal and wild plant foods

Yuma

Geographic Region: Southwest (southeastern California, Colorado River valley)
Linguistic Group: Hokan-Yuman
Principal Dwelling Type: Domed bark, thatch or hide house
Principal Subsistence Type: Maize and other cultivated plants

The Yuma were the dominant tribe in the lower Colorado River valley and gave their name to the linguistic group that encompassed such tribes as the Diegueño, Mojave and Tonto. Their range also once included parts of Arizona and Mexico. By the time of the arrival of Coronado in 1540, they had a well-established agricultural base, and were cultivating large fields of corn and beans, which they irrigated by means of trenches.

In 1985 the total aggregate population of Yuman-speaking peoples, including the Diegueño of California, was 7693.

Yurok

Geographic Region: California (lower Klamath River)
Linguistic Group: Algonquian-Yurok
Principal Dwelling Type:
   Rectangular plank house
Principal Subsistence Type: Mix of animal and wild plant foods, fish

The Yurok were traditionally one of the largest tribes in Northern California and were unique because they were an Algonquian-speaking people. In 1970 there were 959 Yurok in California. In 1985 there were 185 Yurok at Berry Creek, 24 at Big Lagoon, 844 at Resighini, and 69 at the Trinidad Rancheria.

Above left: **A Yurok elder. A custom of this tribe was showing off family wealth, as shown by the dentalium shell skirt worn by the woman (*opposite*)**

Zia Pueblo (*see* Pueblo)

Zuñi

Geographic Region: Southwest
Linguistic Group: Zuñi (related to Uto-Aztecan and Tanoan)
Principal Dwelling Type: Pueblo
Principal Subsistence Type: Maize

The Zuñi, like the Hopi, were linguistically distinct from the Pueblo tribes but related to them culturally. The three groups, Zuñi, Hopi and Pueblo, had several important characteristics in common. First of all, they lived in pueblos (Spanish for village), which were a composite of adobe houses, frequently interconnected and occasionally multistoried, much like a modern apartment complex. While each Pueblo tribe was associated with a single pueblo, the Hopi and Zuñi were each associated with several, and not all members of these tribes lived in pueblos *(see also* Pueblo).

Secondly, the three groups believed in matrilineal descent, by which individuals were associated with the clan of their mother. Thirdly, like the other tribes, the Zuñi had a very complicated religion and tribal hierarchy. The Zuñi hierarchy consisted of four levels, with the rain priests assigned the top rank because rain was an essential factor in their agrarian lifestyle and one which could not always be taken for granted in the Arizona and New Mexico deserts. In addition to maize, the Zuñi traditionally raised beans, squash and melons in irrigated fields.

The Spanish first encountered the Zuñi in 1539, and it is possible that the seven Zuñi pueblos may have been the fabled 'seven golden cities of Cibola' reported by Cabeza de Vaca. Coronado conquered the Zuñi in 1540 and the Spaniards held the land until the Pueblo Revolt of 1680, at which time the seven pueblos were abandoned and their inhabitants merged.

The Zuñi population is said to have stood at 2500 in 1680 as well as in 1950, although it probably had decreased considerably during the nineteenth century. In 1970 it was 5352, and in 1985 the Zuñi Agency and Reservation in New Mexico had a population of 7754.

Above: Agriculture was a skill highly developed within the Zuñi tribe. This photo shows two members planting using the 'waffle bed' method, in which the seeds were placed in holes surrounded by mud walls. These walls kept in water. Gardens took up most of the available land, some growing right up to the house like the pumpkin patch *below*.

Above: Art was another highly prized skill. Paliwahtiwa, Governor of the Zuñi in the late 1880s, wears the elaborate silver and turquoise jewlery commonly found among the tribes of the Southwest. The beaded crescent necklace resembles those of the Navajo. *Page 192:* A Zuñi water jar, circa 1830. This 12-inch jug displays a traditional stylized design.

INDEX

The *Encyclopedia of North American Indian Tribes* presents the tribes in alphabetical order; therefore, the listings given below include references to specific individuals, reservations, important events and other terms that have not been cataloged in the text.

Picture Credits